Francis B. Nyamnjoh
Stories from Abakwa
Mind Searching
The Disillusioned African
The Convert
Souls Forgotten
Married But Available

Dibussi Tande
No Turning Back. Poems of Freedom 1990-1993

Kangsen Feka Wakai
Fragmented Melodies

Ntemfac Ofege
Namondo. Child of the Water Spirits
Hot Water for the Famous Seven
The Return of Omar
Growing Up
Children of Bethel Street

Emmanuel Fru Doh
Not Yet Damascus
The Fire Within
Africa´s Political Wastelands: The Bastardization of Cameroon

Thomas Jing
Tale of an African Woman

Peter Wuteh Vakunta
Grassfields Stories from Cameroon
Green Rape: Poetry for the Environment
Majunga Tok: Poems in Pidgin English
Cry, My Beloved Africa

Ba'bila Mutia
Coils of Mortal Flesh

Kehbuma Langmia
Titabet and the Takumbeng

Victor Elame Musinga
The Barn
The Tragedy of Mr. No Balance

Ngessimo Mathe Mutaka
Building Capacity: Using TEFL and African Languages as
Development-oriented Literacy Tools

Milton Krieger
Cameroon's Social Democratic Front: Its History and Prospects
as an Opposition Political Party, 1990-2011

Sammy Oke Akombi
The Raped Amulet
The Woman Who Ate Python
Beware the Drives: Book of Verse
Susan Nkwentie Nde
Precipice

**Francis B. Nyamnjoh &
Richard Fonteh Akum**
The Cameroon GCE Crisis: A Test of Anglophone Solidarity

Joyce Ashuntantang & Dibussi Tande
Their Champagne Party Will End! Poems in Honor of Bate
Besong
Emmanuel Achu
Disturbing the Peace

Rosemary Ekosso
The House of Falling Women

Peterkins Manyong
God the Politician

George Ngwane
The Power in the Writer: Collected Essays on Culture,
Democracy & Development in Africa

John Percival
The 1961 Cameroon Plebiscite: Choice or Betrayal

Albert Azeyeh
Réussite scolaire, faillite sociale : généalogie mentale de la crise
de l'Afrique noire francophone

Aloysius Ajab Amin & Jean-Luc Dubois
Croissance et développement au Cameroun :
d`une croissance équilibrée à un développement équitable

Carlson Anyangwe
Imperialistic Politics in Cameroun:
Resistance & the Inception of the Restoration of the Statehood
of Southern Cameroons

Excel Tse Chinepoh & Ntemfac A.N. Ofege
The Adventures of Chimangwe

Bill F. Ndi
K`Cracy, Trees in the Storm and Other Poems

**Kathryn Toure, Therese Mungah
Shalo Tchombe & Thierry Karsenti**
ICT and Changing Mindsets in Education

Charles Alobwed'Epie
The Day God Blinked

G.D. Nyamndi
Babi Yar Symphony

Samuel Ebelle Kingue
Si Dieu était tout de chacun?

Ignasio Malizani Jimu
Urban Appropriation and Transformation : bicycle, taxi and
handcart operators in Mzuzu, Malawi

Justice Nyo' Wakai:
Under the Broken Scale of Justice: The Law and My Times

Mediating Legitimacy

Chieftaincy and Democratisation in Two African Chiefdoms

Jude Fokwang

Langaa Research & Publishing CIG
Mankon, Bamenda

Publisher:
Langaa RPCIG
(*Langaa* Research & Publishing Common Initiative Group)
P.O. Box 902 Mankon
Bamenda
North West Province
Cameroon
Langaagrp@gmail.com
www.langaapublisher.com

Distributed outside N. America by African Books Collective
orders@africanbookscollective.com
www.africanbookscollective.com

Distributed in N. America by Michigan State University Press
msupress@msu.edu
www.msupress.msu.edu

ISBN:9956-558-64-8

DISCLAIMER

All views expressed in this publication are those of the author and do not necessarily reflect the views of Langaa RPCIG.

Prologue

In August 2005, I participated at the Pan African Anthropological Association's 15th anniversary conference in Yaoundé, Cameroon. This conference was unique because it devoted a special session on the much-debated question of traditional leadership in Africa, and perhaps unprecedentedly, invited a select number of chiefs from different regions of the continent to share their experiences with scholars researching chieftaincy issues. Three chiefs from the National house of Traditional leaders in South Africa including its chairman flew in for the conference. Chiefs from Benin, Ghana, Nigeria and Cameroon also attended. The session was chaired by Fon Ganyonga III, the traditional leader of the Bali Nyonga chiefdom in the North West province of Cameroon. Fon Ganyonga III is one of the two chiefs examined in this monograph. This event provided an opportunity for traditional leaders to respond to criticisms by scholars dissatisfied with the ways in which some chiefs have positioned themselves in the multi-party era, sometimes at variance with the wishes or interests of their subjects.

Although the session lasted only two or so hours, it achieved in my opinion what its organisers had intended; it enabled the chiefs to engage with scholars and of course provided a continental platform upon which chiefs could interact with each other in addressing issues of common interests. Fon Ganyonga III took the opportunity to invite his South African counterparts to his palace in the chiefdom of Bali Nyonga. During the session, the chiefs re-echoed the claim that they were indeed the true "leaders" on the continent even if they had been pushed to the sidelines of national and continental politics. Whether their rule was legitimate or popular was not the subject of debate, they insisted. They argued instead for the respect of traditional institutions of government and called on national leaders to bring them on board. To this end, they prepared and delivered a motion calling for the establishment of a continental House of Chiefs to complement the existing African Parliament. The importance of a continental House of Chiefs, they argued could not be overemphasised because chiefs can play important roles in the design and implementation of policies that influence the lives of their subjects, particularly rural residents who feel the direct impact of their leadership. Some conference participants responded to this motion with scepticism, choosing instead to raise once again the central question of their legitimacy and relevance in a context of democratisation. The question many had on their mind and that begs to be answered was: what can traditional leaders offer that current democratic models have failed to provide? Put differently, given Africa's desperate attempts to lift its people out of poverty, oppression and corruption, what can chiefs do differently that would contribute to the attainment of people-centred democratic structures and the eradication of poverty? Many see chiefs as part of the problem rather than the solution. In many rural areas across the continent, stories abound of people's lives irreparably scarred by the high-handedness of chiefs determined to get their way at everyone's expense. Others argue that chiefs are worse than politicians because they are not voted into office and therefore cannot be held accountable or voted out, especially in the present dispensation when customary means of curtailing chiefs' powers have waned or been abolished.

Despite these concerns, many chiefs and their supporters maintain that there should be space for them in postcolonial government structures on account of their first-hand knowledge and interaction with rural people. Others have also insinuated that existing plans to inspire an African Renaissance – (however vague the idea) without bringing on board traditional leaders is doomed to fail. What we have noted however, is that since the early 1990s many chiefs across the continent have positioned themselves in the multiparty democratic dispensation as alternative sites of "power" armed with the know-how and legitimacy to seek and defend their people's interests. The resurgence of chiefs – (when many thought their powers would diminish) has been described by some as evidence of "re-traditionalisation" – interpreted possibly as the claim that Africa seems to be under a perpetual spell of tradition and lacks the capacity to dispose of its past – a dark past often associated with monarchical rule that occasionally defies the sophistication and appeal of modernisation. Similarly, others have argued that current dictatorships in Africa and the prolonged stay in power of some leaders such as Omar Bongo, Paul Biya, Robert Mugabe etc - is partly inspired by the monarchical structures embedded in chieftainship. Hence, progress, according to this school of thought is doomed if the question of chieftaincy is not resolved for good – by which they mean its complete eradication. I argue in this volume that it is premature to declare the eradication of chieftaincy and naïve to treat all chieftaincies as embodiments of oppression. Case studies, particularly those that have a comparative framework have the merit of showing the internal logics of these socio-political structures and the ways in which they undermine or contribute to existing democratic structures.

This ethnography revisits the above theme by focusing on the stories of two highly-placed chiefs in two African countries – Cameroon and South Africa. It presents in detail the socio-economic and political contexts in which their leaderships have prevailed and precisely, the kinds of legitimacies they claim for themselves in a post-apartheid context for South Africa, and multi-party era in the case of Cameroon. Analysed as agents, the ethnography depicts the chiefs as social actors endowed with the ability to negotiate multiple kinds of competing relationships with their subjects, local and national governments as well as with other chiefs. Although their socio-economic and political contexts are clearly different, the experiences of both chiefs belie the "re-traditionalisation" thesis espoused by some scholars as a framework for understanding the re-emergence of chiefs in the era of multi-party democracy. Rather, this monograph argues that their actions are informed and mediated largely by existing socio-political realities characteristic of all cultural communities.

Preface

During the 1990s, most African countries experienced what has been termed their 'second independence' (Hyden and Bratton 1992), a period of political upheaval and socio-economic turmoil that led to the introduction of democratic structures across the continent. In many countries including South Africa and Cameroon, the process triggered fresh debates about the status and role of chiefs. The popular assumption in 'struggle circles' such as the African National Congress (ANC) was that chiefs would be relegated to the background in the democratic era, thus giving room to people's power and new forms of accountability. But the introduction of democracy created new conditions where many rural people felt excluded economically from the enchantment and boundless promises of the new dispensation. This dissatisfaction among rural people brought into question the legitimacy of new democratic structures such as the local government even though the ruling ANC continued to enjoy tremendous support among the masses. This in turn provided an enabling environment in which some, but not all chiefs could make new claims for legitimacy. This is because some chiefs remain discredited by their past association with apartheid authorities. Chief Tshivhase of the Tshivhase traditional area in Venda is one of the few chiefs who has successfully associated himself with the ANC both at the national and provincial levels. This has given him scope to act decisively in certain ways on behalf of the poor at the local level, thereby winning credibility among rural people. Thus, his credibility is two-fold – with the national politicians, because he is one of them, and with the rural residents of his chiefdom. Chief Tshivhase's ability to renegotiate his status and gain new legitimacy *as chief* is a particular example of how the emergent game of neo-liberal democracy is played out in post-apartheid South Africa.

In the chiefdom of Bali Nyonga in Cameroon, Chief Ganyonga's career looks rather similar to Tshivhase's insofar as he too has risen to national prominence in the ruling party in Cameroon, the Cameroon People's Democratic Movement (CPDM) in the era of multiparty democracy. But Cameroon's democratic transition was contradictory in the sense that it introduced the form of democracy but not its substance, leaving the ruling party the capacity to manipulate and suppress the opposition and civil society. It was in this context that Ganyonga's prominence in the CPDM contributed to undermining his legitimacy in the eyes of his subjects because they believed that his prominence in the party left them without any shield from the predation and manipulation of the state. Ganyonga was seen to be in 'illicit cohabitation' with a self-serving ruling party, at a time when his subjects wanted to use their newfound rights as citizens to vote the opposition into office. However, Ganyonga's somewhat covert involvement in the politics of the 'Anglophone problem' helped to legitimise his participation in modern politics as a chief.

Against this background, this book examines why both chiefs used their positions as a springboard into national politics? It also establishes the kinds of legitimacy claimed by these chiefs and to what extent the masses are persuaded by such claims and how Tshivhase and Ganyonga's involvement in national politics has affected the relationship between them and their subjects.

This ethnography therefore makes a case for the importance of comparative research on chiefs in the era of democracy and the predicaments they face therein. I argue that contrary to exhortations about the incompatibility of chiefs and democracy, the reality is that political transition in both countries produced contradictions which created space for chiefs to fill but on condition that they were able to draw on different kinds of legitimacy and had not been discredited by their past or present involvement with the postcolonial state.

This study will contribute to existing debates on chieftaincy in Africa, particularly with respect to the sort of relationships they have with their subjects in contexts of socio-economic and political uncertainty. I argue that the institution of chiefship will continue to remain relevant for a range of reasons, not least because of the multiple uses to which it is put by chiefs themselves, the rural masses, local and national politicians and regional elites.

List of Abbreviations

AAC	All Anglophone Conference
ANC	African National Congress
BANDECA	Bali Nyonga Development and Cultural Association
BASCUDA	Bali Social, Cultural and Development Association
BCWC	Bali Community Water Committee
BERCD	Bureau for Economic Research, Cooperation and Development
CODESA	Convention for a Democratic South Africa
CONTRALESA	Congress of Traditional Leaders in South Africa
CPDM	Cameroon People's Democratic Movement
DO	Divisional Officer
DTA	Decentralisation/Traditional Authorities Component
FRELIMO	Frente de Libertação de Moçambique
MIDENO	North West Development Authority
NAIL	New Africa Investment Limited
NOWEFA	North West Fons Association
NOWEFCO	North West Fons Conference
NOWEFU	North West Fons Union
NP	National Party
PAC	Pan African Congress
RENAMO	Resistência Nacional Moçambicana
SACP	South African Communist Party
SADF	South African Defence Force
SANCO	South African National Civic Organisation
SCNC	Southern Cameroons National Council
SDO	Senior Divisional Officer
SNEC	Société Nationale des Eaux du Cameroun
TLC	Transitional Local Council
TTC	Tshivhase Territorial Council
UDC	Union Démocratique Camerounaise
UDF	United Democratic Front
UNC	Union Nationale Camerounaise
UNDP	Union Nationale pour la Démocratie et le Progrès
VDC	Venda Development Corporation
VIPP	Venda Independence People's Party
VNP	Venda National Party

Table of Contents

Acknowledgements

This monograph owes its greatest debt to Prof. John Sharp who negotiated and obtained funding from SANPAD for the project and provided tremendous intellectual support during fieldwork and throughout the period I spent writing up my findings. Prof. Sharp accompanied me during my first trip to Venda and thanks to his networks, I was able to gain easy access to research participants in Venda, particularly, Chief Kennedy Tshivhase, who turned out to be an inspiring person to work with. Chief Tshivhase, a university graduate with a BA in Anthropology readily understood the purpose of my stay in Venda and facilitated my interaction with dozens of his notables and fellow traditional leaders. His mother, Mrs Virginia Tshivhase with whom I shared countless hours of conversation in Thohoyandou proved to be a key asset in my early days of enculturation into the Venda world. She served as my language teacher and despite being a poor student of Tshivenda, she made sure I was able to get by and sometimes, pass for a muVenda. I remain indebted to her patience and hospitality. My research assistant, Saki turned out to be indispensable. He accompanied me to most of the villages and served as my primary interpreter. I also wish to acknowledge the support of Chief Ramugondo who ensured that I had regular access to the weekly meetings in Mukumbani.

In Bali, my father, Mr Fokwang John assisted in facilitating relevant contacts. My uncle, Mr Samuel Kona also made sure I had access to rare documents needed for this project and helped with photocopying. Although I only had access to him towards the end of my fieldwork in Bali, Fon Ganyonga was very supportive of the study and showed remarkable openness during my interview with him.

Two anonymous reviewers provided critical insights that have contributed to the breadth of my analysis. I am profoundly grateful to their criticisms. I wish to thank the following for their direct support towards this project; Mr & Mrs Peter Sama, Francis Fokwang, Emmanuel Ngang, Dema Nukuna (RIP), Divine Fuh, Enos Sikhauli, Mathias Fubah, Pfarelo Matshidze, Ilana van Wyk, Lilian Chenwi, Paul Che, Mufor Atanga, Isak Niehaus and Francis Nyamnjoh. Needless to emphasise that I bear sole responsibility for the deficiencies identified in this work.

Chapter One
Chieftaincy in contemporary perspective

There is another and greater distinction for which no truly natural or religious reason can be assigned, and that is, the distinction of men into Kings and Subjects. Male and female are the distinctions of nature, good and bad the distinctions of heaven; but how a race of men came into the world so exalted above the rest, and distinguished like some new species, is worth enquiring into, and whether they are the means of happiness or of misery to mankind. (Thomas Paine 1995)

Introduction

This book is a comparative study of two African chiefs and chiefdoms in the era of democratisation. It is based on fieldwork in the Tshivhase chiefdom of Venda in South Africa and the chiefdom of Bali-Nyonga in the North West Province of Cameroon. Both studies were conducted between 2001-2002, just over a decade after the so-called democratic transition began in South Africa and in Cameroon. Its main finding is that neither chief has played a marginal role in the politics of the democratic era. Instead - although this is not necessarily true of all the chiefs in their respective countries - both have become involved and prominent in regional and national politics. Particularly interesting is the fact that both chiefs have become involved on the side of the two ruling parties - the African National Congress (ANC) in South Africa and the Cameroon Peoples' Democratic Movement (CPDM) in Cameroon. Drawing on this parallel, I examine the following questions: Why in both cases have these chiefs used their positions as a springboard into national politics? Why have both decided to become involved in the political structures of the ruling parties? What effect have their decisions in this regard had on their relationships with their subjects? What do the answers to these questions tell us about the 'democratic transition' in South Africa and Cameroon, and more profoundly about the nature of the South African and Cameroon postcolonial states?

Generally, most ethnographic studies on chieftaincy have focused on single field sites. Except for the recent comparative study of chiefs in Cameroon and Botswana by Nyamnjoh (2002), not much attention has been given to this form of inquiry. Comparison is vital in the social sciences in order to 'explore the varieties of forms of social life as a basis for the theoretical study of human social phenomena' (Radcliffe-Brown 1958:108). In the past, Radcliffe-Brown contends, the comparative method in social anthropology was often used by 'arm-chair anthropologists', but the emergence of field studies gradually marginalized the need for a comparative method. However, an increasing number of social scientists have felt the need to embark on comparative studies principally because 'factual information about one society, of course, will not always tell us whether we are dealing with an unusual case or a very general set of influences' (Giddens 2001:639). In fact, some scholars are of the opinion that the substance of the social sciences remains the comparative method.

However, before we go into the details of the foregoing questions, I wish to draw on an event witnessed towards the end of my fieldwork in Venda, which I reckon encapsulates the essence of the issues I will address in this book. On the 23rd of August 2001 hundreds of civic members from urban and rural areas in the Thulamela municipality marched on the council premises in Thohoyandou (capital of the Vhembe district council) to protest against the council authorities. I found this incident interesting because the new council had been in office for less than a year. The council had taken over from the Transitional Local Councils (TLCs) in December 2000. During the protest march, civic members sang anti-council slogans and passed a vote of no confidence on council authorities. Among their grievances, the civic members emphasised their disappointment with the management style of the council. Civic members from rural areas in particular pointed out that the council should desist from charging a fee from rural dwellers in return for services because most people could not afford to pay. Protesters delivered a memorandum, which spelt out their collective grievances although emphasis was on the immediate concerns of the urban residents. Among other things, the civics demanded that 'the inefficient, selfish, undemocratic and insensitive council should disband and vacate their offices as from August 25, 2001.'[1] They appealed to the Executive Mayor of the Vhembe District Council to oversee a transitional period while a 'new democratic council' was brought into place. They also called for the unconditional scrapping of all outstanding debts with immediate effect, citing the reason that the municipality had falsely issued statements demanding payment for services that had not been rendered;

> Today we have decided enough is enough against the municipality who do not respond to our concerns as community. We, the people of the above-mentioned areas, together with our civic and traditional leaders, have noted that there is sheer inefficiency in the municipality. Letters and submissions dating many months back go unanswered without even acknowledgement of receipts, which is a sign of arrogance. This belies the ... principles of democracy and transparency.' (Memorandum of Civics, August 23, 2001, Thohoyandou).

It should be emphasised that the civic members were not opposed to democratic local government as such, but resented the way in which the council conducted its affairs. Protesters isolated in particular, the mayor and other council officials and accused them of corruption:

> There are clear signs of corruption wherein a few individuals benefit at the expense of the poor. Many of them shamelessly disadvantage some areas unduly, to the benefit of the specific areas where they stay or come from, (Memorandum of Civics, August 23, 2001).

Municipal authorities were also accused of fixing rates without consultation with the civic members of the different locations and villages. The protesters claimed that the council had raised the rates arbitrarily in order to 'cover up for the massive financial losses resulting from corruption.' Rural dwellers in particular expressed their support for traditional rulers who were being marginalised by the municipal authorities. In this respect, civic members called on the future council to include chiefs in all processes of decision-making when issues affecting rural areas were under discussion. Finally, they maintained that they were going to boycott the payment of rates and bills until the council had arrived at an amicable settlement with them:

We also like you to know that our constituencies would not pay any bill from the same municipality until our demands are met. We adhere without reservation to a thinking that due rates should be paid regularly. However, we hold strongly that such rates should be proportional to the services rendered and they should be an outcome of such sufficient consultation as may be expected in democracy. (Memorandum of Civics, 23rd August 2001).

Although this protest march was unprecedented in Venda, it should be pointed out that dissatisfaction with local government initially emerged during the period of the TLC. This dissatisfaction was especially serious among rural civic members who felt betrayed by the TLC for charging fees for services that had not been delivered and for its unpopular policy over the allocation of land in rural areas (discussed in chapter three). These developments gave rise to a situation where the rural poor needed protection from market forces and as seen above, the local council could not provide such protection. On the contrary, they were keen on drawing the rural poor closer into its market-driven policy. It was against this background that so-called traditional authorities benefited from and made use of the unpopularity of the municipal council. The main beneficiaries of the council's unpopularity were Chief Tshivhase and most of the headmen under him.

This is evidenced by some of Chief Tshivhase's actions as well as those of his headmen. In this respect, he did not only stand up to the council's attempt to take over land allocation in his chiefdom but he also kept the charges for this service lower than the municipal council. Tshivhase also opened access of land to women and introduced the Tshivhase Development Trust as an alternative arm of development in his chiefdom. The effects of these developments are many. One of them was that civic organisations began to co-operate with the chief and his headmen thereby reducing their hostility towards traditional leaders, which began during the struggles in the 1980s. This co-operation was mainly in the form of attending meetings hosted by chiefs and restyling these meetings along the line of 'people's forums'.

There is something ironic about these developments. The current amicable relationship between civic organisations in Tshivhase and the chiefs belies the situation in the 1980s. The relationship between chiefs and civic organisations in the 1980s was characterised by ruthless hostility. This antagonism is to a large extent, an issue of the past in Tshivhase. Thus, a question worth posing is: what has brought about these changes? Why in the democratic era, has the chief become a central political figure in the chiefdom? It should be borne in mind that my observations in Tshivhase are not necessarily true in other chiefdoms in South Africa, or even in Venda. I have evidence that other chiefs in Venda have not been able to rehabilitate themselves as successfully as Chief Tshivhase. Evidence for this will be produced and analysed in chapters three and six.

The situation in Bali Nyonga was different from that in Tshivhase. In fact, the reverse of what was happening in Tshivhase was taking place in Bali. Unlike in Tshivhase where the chief had gained popularity for offering protection to his people against the local council, in Bali the people resented the fact that the chief had joined the ranks of the ruling party, thereby leaving them at the mercy of the predatory state. In other words, people felt betrayed by the fact that instead of providing them with shield against the government, Ganyonga was perceived to have become a facilitator or a tool in the hands of the government against them. In order to put this view into perspective, let me draw on a particular incident observed during fieldwork. On 28 January 2002, the Senior Divisional Officer (SDO) for Mezam division visited Bali on an official tour. Judging by the massive turn out and the prestige enjoyed by the fon[2] during the occasion, one could be driven to guess that he was in harmony with his subjects. During the SDO's visit, normal business was disallowed, which entailed the closure of government offices, shops and schools. Pupils and students from both government and private schools all flocked to the grand stand where the SDO was scheduled to address the people. Members of political parties had put aside their differences, albeit momentarily, and came out in their numbers, ostensibly to show their relative worth in terms of militants. In brief, the SDO's visit vividly captured the totality of local relations in Bali. All the local actors were present, the chief and his notables, the mayor, political parties and their local leaders, party militants and ordinary subjects as well as local government officials. The visit was hailed as a major success and was reported in the local press and the government-controlled *Radio Bamenda*.

Despite this semblance of harmony, many were displeased that the SDO's visit had been scheduled on the customary "market day", thereby disrupting a complex trading system that drew its time-honoured sustenance from inter-chiefdom activities. In the grassfields of Bamenda, each chiefdom devoted a day during the week for its market-day. This day was not fixed, but rotated according to the traditional calendar of the chiefdom. In most cases, the day preceding the market day was considered as the chiefdom's sacred day of rest or what is commonly known as 'Kontri Sunday'. The success of each market day did not only depend on the participation of the local population but to a large extent, on people from other towns and neighbouring chiefdoms who came to sell their articles and buy local products.

Owing to the SDO's intended visit to Bali on its market day, the Traditional Council, headed by the chief had decided to move the market date a day earlier in order to enable people with the time to welcome the SDO. Although Bali residents complied with this legislation, they resented the fact that the chief was unable to stand up to the SDO and protect their interests. Apparently, the market day was poorly attended due to the sudden change. Informants pointed out that the chief should have obliged the SDO to visit a day earlier or much later in order not to disrupt the people's economic activities. Others blamed the chief for allowing himself to be manipulated by petty government administrators such as the SDO, in contrast to his late father, the former chief, Galega II, who had commanded tremendous respect in the entire region – a claim substantiated by an official visit to his palace by the former state president, Ahmadou Ahidjo. Although the above incident may appear trivial to an outsider, it should be emphasised that two specific issues were of paramount concern to the people. First, the chief's perceived inability to control the tide of events in his chiefdom was interpreted by his subjects as a weakness on his part and on the other hand, it also confirmed the claim that having failed to protect them, they had increasingly become subject to the whims and caprices of the state and its stooges.

Similar to the case in Tshivhase, several questions could be posed drawing on the incident recounted above: what has brought about these changes? Why in the era of democracy has the chief become unpopular? What legitimacy has the chief retained or

[4]

claimed, who is persuaded and why? One note however. It should be observed that unlike the case in Tshivhase, which is more or less unique in Venda, chief Ganyonga's experience represents to a large extent, the predicament faced by other traditional rulers in the Bamenda grassfields in the present era. I shall refer to and analyse some of these cases in chapters five and six.

The two cases above provide a basis for comparison, a key objective of this work. A question worth posing in this regard is whether Cameroon is following the predictions about the incompatibility of chiefs and democracy, whereas South Africa is not? Although it appears so, I wish to suggest that issues are actually much more complex than this, as will become evident in chapters five and six. The comparative part of the book shall focus on the following variables: i) the status of chiefs in the democratic era, ii) the kinds of legitimacy claimed by chiefs, iii) and the nature of the democratic transition in both countries. It is intended that this enterprise shall make a case for the importance of comparative work in the social sciences in general and on the question of chiefs and democratisation in Africa in particular.

Areas of Study

As indicated above, the study was conducted in two African chiefdoms-Tshivhase in South Africa and Bali Nyonga in Cameroon. Tshivhase is one of the 25 recognised Venda chiefdoms in the Limpopo Province. Venda is one of the nine former black homelands in South Africa, which was known between 1979 and 1994 as the Republic of Venda. It spans the area from longitude 29o40' E. to 30o 50' E. and latitude 22o 20' S. to 23o 10' S. in Limpopo Province in South Africa. The chiefdom of Tshivhase is the most populated and largest chiefdom in the Limpopo Province.[3]

Figure 1: Maps of South Africa and the Tshivhase area

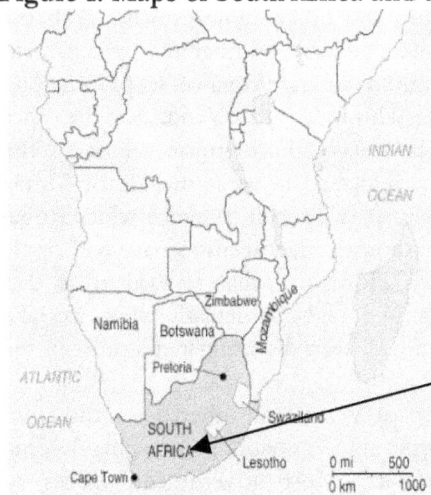

South Africa
Vendaland –Tshivhase

The chiefdom of Tshivhase is headed by Chief Kennedy Tshivhase who came to the throne in 1970 at the age of eight following the sudden death of his father in a car accident. Owing to his tender age, his uncle was installed as regent to manage the affairs of the chiefdom. Kennedy Tshivhase regained his office in 1993, a year before the Republic of Venda was reincorporated into South Africa. Kennedy Tshivhase studied at the University of the North near Polokwane (formerly Pietersburg) in the 1980s. He earned a

Bachelor's degree in Anthropology and rose to prominence in the early 1990s following his appointment to a cabinet post by the Venda military leader, Gabriel Ramushwana. After Venda was re-incorporated into South Africa, Kennedy Tshivhase was appointed to the House of Senate in Cape Town. He was re-deployed in 1997 to the Limpopo Provincial Legislature as an ANC Member, a position he held until 2005.

The population of Venda was estimated at 542 000 in 1990 with an unemployment rate of 34.8% - the highest in the 'independent' homelands.[4] Personal monthly income per capita for Venda was R59, which was also the lowest when compared to the rates in the other independent homelands.[5] These statistics reveal not only the socio-economic predicament of the citizens of Venda during its period of 'independence' but also the challenges they faced after Venda's re-integration into the Republic of South Africa. This predicament was not restricted to Venda alone. The Limpopo Province was one of the least developed in the new South Africa. The 1996 census revealed that up to 50% of people over 15 years of age in the province were illiterate. Furthermore, 50% of the economically active population was unemployed.[6]

Although substantial attempts were made to implement development projects for Venda citizens, it is evident from the statistics above and my observations in the field that the bulk of the population lives in poverty. During Venda's 'independence' from South Africa, the Venda Development Corporation (VDC) was established as the principal agent of development. Its main objective was 'to erect, plan, finance, co-ordinate, promote, relocate and continue industrial, commercial, financial, mining and other business enterprises' in the Venda territory (BERCD 1979:68-9). The VDC also built hundreds of houses for the civil servants and the emerging elite in Thohoyandou, the capital of the Venda Republic.

Venda was not (and is still not) highly industrialised due partly to what some have described as its 'unfavourable location,' although a few industries were located in Shayandima, an area next to Thohoyandou, where over a thousand citizens were employed. During the homeland period, Venda was also a labour reserve for the industries and mines principally in Johannesburg and other mining towns. With the demise of the apartheid State and the consequent influx of migrants to the main metropolitan areas of South Africa – such as in the Gauteng Province, employers tend to recruit available labourers resident in Gauteng. This means that Venda, like the other homelands is no longer perceived as a labour reserve. Furthermore, most of the industries in Shayandima have closed down or relocated to areas outside of Venda territory triggering a sharp rise in unemployment. It is difficult to gauge which 'tribal authority' was affected most by these transformations as they seem to have had ripple effects throughout the entire Venda territory. However, what is evident is that unemployment in the Tshivhase area was extremely high, particularly when we take into account the fact that people from this area had been discriminated against in the civil service during Mphephu's presidency.[7]

It therefore seems that the re-incorporation of Venda and other homelands into South Africa triggered substantial socio-economic transformation, sometimes leading to increased poverty and economic uncertainty. Most government offices in Thohoyandou closed down after 1994, owing to the fact that Venda was incorporated into the Northern Province (now Limpopo), which has its administrative headquarters at Polokwane. This situation of 'economic crisis' is not unrelated to the emergence and popularity of prosperity gospel churches such as the Universal Church of God based in Thohoyandou (see Comaroff and Comaroff 1999b for similarities in the North West province of South Africa; and Matshidze 2003 on the Universal Church of God in Thohoyandou). Clearly, the above issues are central for a proper understanding of this ethnography.

The other area considered in this study is the chiefdom of Bali Nyonga. Commonly known as Bali, it is one of the five 'first class' chiefdoms[8] in the North West Province of Cameroon located in longitude 10° 4' East and latitude 5° 54' North. Bali is a sub-division in Mezam Division of the North West Province with an estimated population of 75000. The chiefdom is located 16km south west of Bamenda, the provincial capital. Its neighbours to the south are the chiefdoms of Pinyin, Asong and Guzang and to the east are the Baforchu, Alatening and Mbatu. The chiefdom of Bali consists of 54 quarters and five villages including five sub-chiefs.

The fon of Bali, Dohsang Galega, was crowned on 6 October 1985 following the 'disappearance'[9] of his father, fon Galega II. On his accession to office, he chose to be crowned with the regnal name, Ganyonga III. Ganyonga studied in Cameroon and Germany where he earned a doctorate in Sociology shortly before he assumed office. In 1990 Ganyonga and two other prominent fons of the grassfields were appointed into the Central Committee of the ruling party, the CPDM. He has occupied this position to date and has been active in regional and national politics. He also lectured Sociology at the *Ecole Normal Superieur,* a school of the University of Yaoundé 1 at Bambili.

The Cameroon government has no recent statistics for the country or Bali specifically which, regrettably, leaves enormous room for conjecture. Consequently, I shall rely on general statistics on Cameroon and my personal observations in the field. Like Venda, the North West Province has only a few primary industries with a small percentage of the population employed as civil servants. National unemployment as estimated in 2001 stands at 30% and 70% of the labour force is occupied in the agricultural sector as opposed to 13% in industry and commerce.[10] My estimate is that about 70% of the population in Bali are peasants and as such, predominantly peasant farmers. Although a small percentage of the people are civil servants, most of them practise subsistence farming in order to supplement their income and engage in trade within and between neighbouring chiefdoms.

Figure 2: Political map of Cameroon

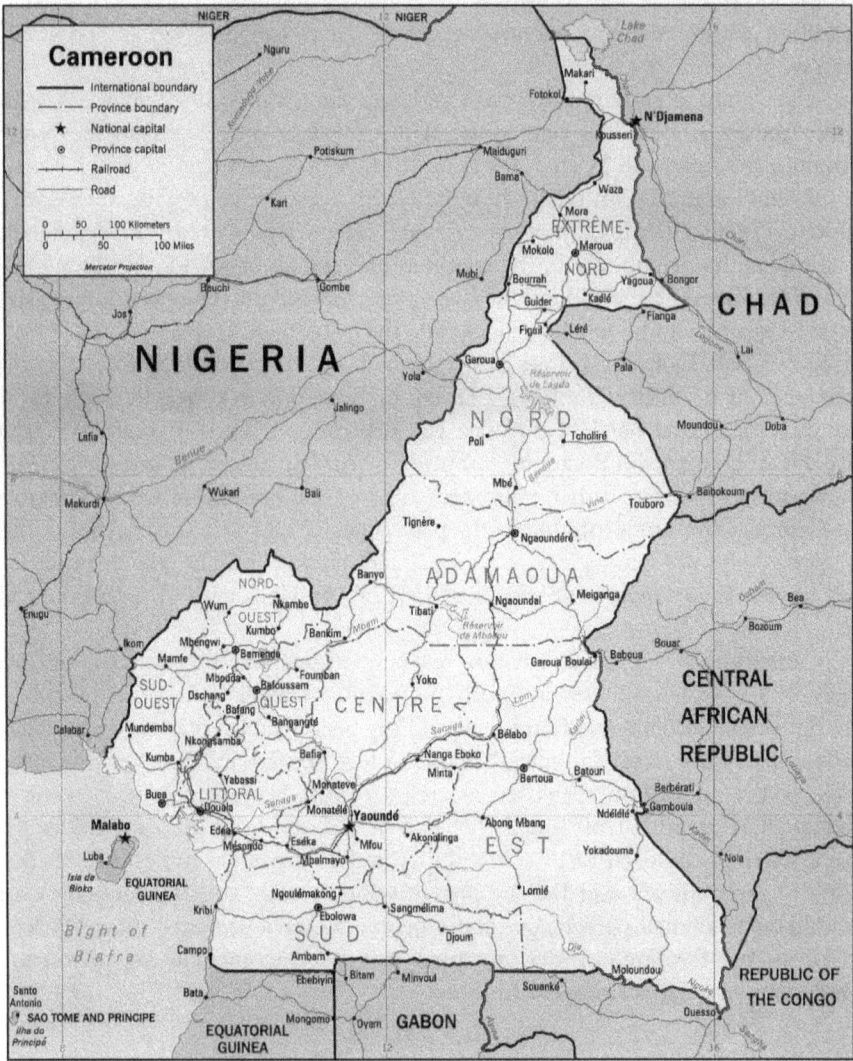

Chiefs and Democracy: Strange bedfellows?

In this section, I examine some of the key works and theoretical approaches that have informed current debates on chieftaincy in South Africa and Cameroon. At issue is the prediction about the incompatibility of chiefs and democracy. Although not new, this view has been articulated quite aptly by Govan Mbeki (1984) in his book *The Peasants Revolt* in which he argued in the 1980s that 'if the Africans have had chiefs, it was because all human societies have had them at one stage or another. But when a people have developed to a stage which discards chieftainship, when their social development contradicts the need for such an institution, then to force it on them is not liberation but enslavement' (Mbeki 1984:47). It was in this light that many 'freedom fighters' anticipated the demise of the institution of chieftaincy alongside apartheid. Even after 1994, many activists felt that chiefs would be relegated to the background and eventually lose their legitimacy (cf. Maloka 1996). Although this view was not as popular in Cameroon as in South Africa, some Cameroonians felt quite strongly that chiefs and democracy were incompatible. For instance, a commentator in a local newspaper argued that 'by their calling and function, traditional rulers are ultra-conservatives, who misjudge challenges for contempt, consider new ideas as anathema, and are allergic and uptight to liberal changes. Their static mental structure set do (sic) not permit any opening to democracy which is a form of modern participatory governance incompatible with their archaic perceptions.'[11]

Thus the debate on chiefs and democracy as framed in this study concerns the view that chiefs are at best irrelevant and incompatible with the democratic model. This debate could be divided into two broad categories. On the one hand those who hold the opinion that chieftaincy should be eradicated completely in preference for democratic rule because chieftaincy is not only outmoded, but it has also been corrupted by processes of state formation, colonialism and apartheid. On the other hand, we have those who argue, (activists and researchers) that chiefs and democracy are not incompatible. They maintain that chiefs are intercalary categories, located between the state and their rural communities and should be understood in terms of the complexities surrounding the postcolonial state. A third category constitutes those who hold essentialist ideas about the compatibility of chiefs and democracy. This camp maintains that chieftaincy represents a 'true' African form of democracy and should be considered alongside modern forms of liberal democracy.

An important work which has spelt out the different positions of the current debate on chieftaincy is West and Kloeck-Jenson's (1999) article on traditional authority and democratic decentralisation in post-war Mozambique. Although their article is limited to Mozambique, it reflects much of the debate that currently prevails in South Africa, and to a limited extent, Cameroon. The debate surrounding chieftaincy in Mozambique, West and Kloeck-Jenson contend, has gained momentum since former President Joaquim Chissano's declaration in 1995 that his government desired the existence of traditional authorities. This statement contradicted a long-standing government policy that had abolished chieftaincy immediately after independence. Despite this new and amicable approach to traditional leadership, current political debate in Mozambique is divided into two opposing camps. On the one hand, there is the *Frente de Libertação de Moçambique* (FRELIMO), which argues that chiefs have been 'compromised' as a result of their association with the colonial state and consequently, have no role or place in the postcolonial and new democratic dispensation. FRELIMO accused the chiefs of having facilitated colonialism (through taxation, labour conscription and policing) and also of having benefited enormously from it and accumulated power for themselves. Thus, FRELIMO's victory against the Portuguese was also interpreted as a victory against chiefs (*autoridades gentilicas*). Chiefs were therefore 'systematically excluded from positions of responsibility' in the postcolonial era and replaced with *grupos dinamizadores* (dynamizing groups).

On the other hand, there are those who contend that traditional authority epitomises a 'genuinely African form of local governance.' This position has been championed by two groups in Mozambique. First, the *Resistência Nacional Moçambicana* (RENAMO) has advocated 'a return to the pre-independence state of affairs in which local chiefs had been respected and obeyed' (West and Kloeck-Jenson 1999:460). Second, the 'Decentralisation/Traditional Authorities Component' (DTA) of the Ministry of State Administration has increasingly advocated the revival of traditional authority in rural Mozambique. According to West and Kloeck-Jensen, the DTA research director Iraê Lundin argued in one of her publications that traditional authority or what she calls 'African Local Authority' could be seen as a 'sociocultural affirmation of Africanness' (ibid. 473).

West and Kloeck-Jenson argue however, that 'history powerfully illustrates the fallacy of these over-simplifications' (ibid. 474). They maintain that chieftaincy has different meanings for different localities. In the north of Mozambique, for example, 'kin-based systems of authority' have been incorporated into 'larger and larger regimes including … the colonial state,' (ibid. 475) and their functions have changed with the regimes as well. Thus, there is nothing particularly genuine or 'African' about traditional authority as romanticised by the government-sponsored research project. Hence West and Kloeck-Jenson conclude that in Mozambique, 'chiefs at all levels have occupied positions betwixt and between their populations and higher authorities, implicating them all in a history of extraction and violence larger than all concerned' (ibid. 475). According to them, the important questions to pose in any current study of chieftaincy are: who claims 'legitimacy', by what argument, who is persuaded and why? Though these questions address specific issues in Mozambique, they also raise issues relevant to our understanding of chieftaincy in Tshivhase and Bali. For instance, one may also pose the above questions about chiefs in Tshivhase – namely, who claims legitimacy, by what argument, who is persuaded and why?

Following the contours of the debate suggested above, I will proceed to examine Mahmood Mamdani's position outlined in his celebrated book *Citizens and Subjects* (1996). In many respects, *Citizens and Subjects* is much about chieftaincy as well as a solid analysis of democratisation and the state in Africa. According to him, what is particularly interesting about chieftaincy today is not what some may perceive as the 'continuity of tradition', but precisely what he sees as the 'break in continuity' (Mamdani 1996:43). According to him, chieftaincy exists today not as a result of its own legitimacy, but because of its cooperation with (and simultaneous corruption by) the colonial and apartheid states. Mamdani belongs to the camp that strongly advocates the eradication of chieftaincy in the postcolonial state. According to him, contemporary chieftaincy is in many respects a category of 'decentralised despotism' (as it was during the colonial state) owing to the withering away of institutionalised mechanisms that served to check the chief against excesses. Prior to colonial rule, the chief was the custodian of land not its proprietor and 'the ultimate popular sanction against a despotic chief was desertion.' But under colonial and apartheid rule, the powers of the chief were systematically strengthened - emphasising the state as the 'determiner of the consensus' (Mamdani 1996:45). These transformations led to the bifurcation of the state not only into racialised categories, but also into the categories of 'citizen' and 'subject'. On the one hand the lives of subjects were regulated by chiefs under customary law, and on the other hand the lives of citizens were regulated by modern law. And the tragic tale, according to him, is that most postcolonial states in Africa succeeded to deracialise but not to democratise the bifurcated state, thereby maintaining the basic framework of decentralised despotism to the detriment of the rural peasantry. Mamdani's panacea is to eradicate the institution of chief, which represents and propagates the bifurcated world of citizens and subjects. By introducing democratic reforms which encompass the worlds of both citizens and subjects, the urban and the rural, the central, and the local, African states can be sure of a world entirely of citizens, no longer bifurcated and despotic. In fact, Mamdani's position on the eradication of chieftaincy now seems to be favoured by some international development agencies who perceive the institution as an 'irredeemably illiberal institution' even when African governments seem to offer support for it (Fanthorpe 2005:28).

The strength of Mamdani's argument lies, in my opinion, in his exploration of the historical trends chieftaincy has undergone and the extent of the debt contemporary chieftaincy owes its colonial and apartheid legacies. However, his theoretical approach not only falls short of explaining the continued role of chiefs in many rural areas of South Africa and the rest of the continent, but also overlooks the fact that people tend to straddle the dual identities of citizen and subject.

Mamdani is not alone in calling for the eradication of chieftaincy in South Africa. In his article, 'Traditional Leaders and the Current Transition' Maloka (1995) argues that chieftaincy in contemporary South Africa is in all respects an outmoded institution in dire need of being replaced by democratic institutions. To him, most of those laying claim to the status of chief are no more than former bantustan petty bourgeois 'hoping to further their own careers in the new dispensation by exploiting "tradition"' (Maloka 1995:35). He sees the post-apartheid state in South Africa as a 'contested terrain not only between forces representing the former white interests and those of the liberation movement, but also between different fractions of the black petty bourgeoisie' (ibid. 173-4). On account of their innumerable *sins* of commission or omission, Maloka insists, chiefs should be limited to playing an advisory and ceremonial role in elected local government structures. Furthermore, he calls for 'progressive forces' to co-ordinate a 'clear political campaign' that seeks to 'reduce the material basis for the legitimacy of chieftaincy' (1995:39). Maloka sees the demise of chieftaincy as part and parcel of the consolidation of democratic structures. He anticipates that it will not be chiefs but rather the newly established local governments in South Africa that will extend 'popular participation to the local level.'

Like Mamdani, Maloka tends to treat chiefs as a homogeneous category. According to his logic, all chiefs have been implicated in the violence and extraction of the colonial and apartheid era and should therefore be excluded from participating in the new democratic dispensation. Although Maloka's perspective illustrates the ability of chiefs to engage in modern politics, his theoretical approach ironically empties chiefs of agency, thereby presenting them as passive and residual entities, ripe for eradication. It is doubtful to what extent his call for 'progressive forces' to historicize and undermine the legitimacy of chiefs will be worthwhile, given his reluctance to conceptualise chiefs as political actors who will not sit back to watch the demise of the institution.

This notwithstanding, Mamdani and Maloka's approaches have several interesting and worthy claims, such as the observation that colonial and apartheid regimes despoiled and abused the institution of chief (see Geschiere 1993 for parallels in East Cameroon). But most of their discussions are based on scholarship that is not grounded on extensive ethnographic inquiry. Their theories tell us little about the relationship between chiefs and the people on the ground today, nor do they demonstrate that the alternatives they advocate are any better. For example, Maloka's (1995) call for an agenda that aims to erode the legitimacy of chiefs and to replace them with democratic structures fails to ask or reflect on the following: i) how 'democratic' are the new supposedly democratic structures on the ground? ii) What is the relationship between chiefs and these democratic structures? iii) Have so-called democratic structures actually managed or controlled access to strategic resources such as land to the satisfaction of the target population? Later in this work, I will throw more light on these issues and show to what extent selected chiefs are grappling with such matters in the post-apartheid era.

Much of the current literature provides evidence for the compatibility of chiefs and democracy (Becker 2006; Friedman 2005; Gonçalves 2005; Lindstrom and White 1997; Oomen 2005). Evidence for this is based on research and discussions on policy frameworks affecting chiefs, the role of chiefs in rural local government and their involvement in regional and or national politics. Ntsebeza (1998; 2005) for instance has examined the predicament of chiefs in the new South Africa following legislation that has affected the institution since the early 1990s. He points out that the South African Constitution and the Local Government Transition Act of 1993 (as amended), 'do not anticipate any meaningful role for traditional authorities in local government.' According to him, there is an obvious difference in opinion between the older generation and the younger generation with regard to the question of constitutional guarantees for traditional leadership. While the older generation, for instance represented by Nelson Mandela, supports the view that chieftaincy should gain more constitutional accommodation, the younger camp, represented by the South African National Civic Organisation (SANCO), youths and the South African Communist Party (SACP) maintains that chieftaincy should be restricted to *custom* and *tradition*, or better still, eradicated completely.

Bank and Southall (1996) have interesting findings with respect to the status of chiefs in post-apartheid South Africa. In addition to exploring the policy framework dealing with chiefs, they argue that traditional leadership does not necessarily contradict democracy. To them, traditional leadership can in fact 'provide the bedrock upon which to construct new and experimental governments, including constitutional democracies.' They also consider an important question ignored by Maloka (1995) and Mamdani (1996): *what is the relationship between chiefs and new democratic structures on the ground in the countryside?* In answer, they provide ethnographic data from Mpumalanga, which they claim demonstrate that 'chiefly courts and people's courts co-exist at the local level.' But this is not necessarily true of all areas and their investigations in the Eastern Cape reveal a different trend. The Eastern Cape is characterised by continuous struggle between traditional leaders and civic organisations. This bitter struggle has led to kidnappings, politically-motivated assaults and murders (see Lodge 1999 for more on this conflict). According to Bank and Southall, there is no contradiction between chieftaincy and democracy. Mamdani and Maloka, just like the FRELIMO-led government in Mozambique, observe that chiefs have been corrupted by colonial rule and apartheid, and should be excluded from competing with the new elite of the postcolonial state, especially in the democratic era. Bank and Southall argue that chieftaincy as such does not contradict democracy and proceed to show how the institution is capable of collaborating with democratic structures on the ground, thereby contributing to democracy as a whole.

Nkuna's (2002) study is also worth reviewing, particularly because he carried out his research at the same time as mine although in a different municipality in South Africa. His study demonstrates the tensions between the Tzaneen municipal council and the rural citizens following what he calls the 'municipalisation' of rural communities without consultation with the masses. He focuses on three villages; Dan, Petanenge and Khujwana, which were incorporated into the Greater Tzaneen municipality in 1997. According to him, the Tzaneen TLC began by demanding payments for services and resources. The council is alleged to have issued water bills to citizens ranging from R60 to R450. This situation was absurd given that many people received bills despite the fact that they did not have water installations in their stands. He also claims that in some of the villages, citizens were requested to pay between R20 and R50 for the municipal cemetery and between R50 to R80 for the maintenance of the road networks (ibid. 65-70).

In a dramatic event, the civic members and headmen of Dan village invited the chief and local government officials to an important meeting to explain the developments to the community. The chief was also accused of having sold a piece of their communal land to the TLC for the construction of pay-points in the villages. Although government officials failed to attend the meeting, the chief denied the accusations and argued instead that he had similar grudges as his subjects, against the municipal council. The chief insisted that he had not been consulted before the implementation of the municipal council's policies in his chiefdom. He then used the opportunity to urge his subjects not to pay for any services.

Nkuna observes that the chief's intervention resulted in the people's refusal to cooperate with the municipal authorities. In Dan village for example, most people denied access to the municipal construction workers either by locking their gates or by verbally insulting them to back off. In some neighbourhoods of the village where meters had already been installed, the people alleged that the meters had been stolen, thereby incapacitating the municipal council. Eventually the municipal authorities were forced to discontinue the provision of services such as the installation of water. From the viewpoint of the people, the problem was not that they were resisting development but because the municipal authorities had failed to consult them or had any intentions of doing so in future. They also resented the fact that the municipal authorities sought to treat them in the same way as urban dwellers, irrespective of their socio-economic predicament. It should be pointed out that there are striking parallels between Nkuna's study and this work. I shall make use of his findings in chapter three below to substantiate my argument on the tensions between local government and the rural poor and the position of chiefs therein.

Barbara Oomen's (2000; 2002; 2005) research in the Mamone chiefdom in Limpopo Province reveals an unprecedented upsurge in discourse about the renewed importance of chieftaincy as an emblem of African 'tradition.' After the collapse of the apartheid state, she contends, which sought to despoil and deny the Africans their 'culture', people are now 'going back to their roots', to their history in search of a rebirth or 'renaissance' (to borrow from the current catchphrase). She refers to this upsurge as *retraditionalisation* and supports her argument with several statistics, one of which is a 73% support for the institution of chief in Mamone. Despite this enormous 'support' for chieftaincy, she contends, there is an ongoing contest over what role the chief should play in rural local government. This, she asserts, is evidence that 'tradition is far from fixed, but constantly redebated at the local level.'

Oomen's study reveals three main issues about the situation of chiefs in post-apartheid South Africa: a) that chiefs are highly organised through a central organisation, the Congress of Traditional Leaders in South Africa (CONTRALESA) that represents their interests. b) that chiefs are still perceived as 'vote brokers' in rural areas and c) that alternative institutions - that is, the newly created local councils are often lacking in strength and experience to perform their functions.

Although Oomen's conclusions resonate with my own research, her concept of 'retraditionalisation' seems deficient. The claims embodied in 'retraditionalisation' sound quite similar to the DTA project's romanticised notion of chieftaincy as an affirmation of 'Africanness' and indigenous African democracy (West and Kloeck-Jensen 1999). Clearly, her approach does not see tradition as a fixed category, but the notion of retraditionalisation conveys the idea of recourse to a specific, predefined set of practices known as 'tradition'. In addition, retraditionalisation may also imply that despite colonialism and apartheid's attempts to 'modernise' and transform Africans from their 'backward' cultures to modern and 'progressive' individuals, they have opted instead to go back to their roots – however elusive these roots are, thereby contradicting the modernisation project. Oomen's concept of retraditionalisation is therefore not only ambiguous, but also runs the risk of implying that chieftaincy is synonymous with the essence of 'Africanness'.

In Cameroon, especially in the North West Province, much of the literature on chiefs and democracy has focussed on the coping strategies of chiefs in the current era. But a striking difference from South Africa is that arguments for undermining or eradicating chieftaincy in the democratic era have hardly been raised in political or academic circles. On the contrary, a different kind of debate is prevalent, echoes of which have begun to emerge in South Africa (see Mashele 2004), specifically that in order to maintain their legitimacy as custodians of "tradition", chiefs should distance themselves from party politics. Although there are several positions, I have delimited the discussion to two principal axes around which the debate revolves. On the one hand, a majority of subjects and the main opposition party, the Social Democratic Front (SDF) advocate that chiefs should be 'neutral' in party politics – that is, they should not publicly express, or identify with particular kinds of political opinion or choices, because they command a following that incorporates people with diverse and sometimes conflicting political inclinations. On the other hand, certain chiefs and some militants of the ruling Cameroon Peoples' Democratic Movement (CPDM) have maintained that chiefs, as citizens, have a constitutional right to membership and to be active in any party of their choice. Although easy as it may appear, the various positions outlined above are in fact more nuanced and plural – positions that will come under sharp focus in chapter five.

Peter Geschiere has devoted close to three decades of research on the interaction between local communities and the postcolonial state in various parts of Cameroon and, consequently, has contributed a great deal to the debate on chiefs especially in the post-1990 era. Since 1990, he argues, there is a demand for political actors of a new kind in Cameroon. He asks if these changes (that is, the struggle for the introduction of democratic reforms) will not create conditions for the return of old political actors such as chiefs into the 'national political scene'. He anticipates quite rightly that 'democratisation and elections might ...offer new chances to old political actors' such as 'customary authorities', but wonders if they have 'retained sufficient prestige to function as vote banks in the new setting' (Geschiere 1993:151).

From his study of chiefs among the Maka of South-East Cameroon and the Bakweri of the South West Province, he concludes that 'the present-day position of chiefs is marked by a strong ambivalence, even in areas where their power does have deeper historical roots' (ibid. 152). This is because they 'seem to represent "tradition", but at the same time the State uses them to further "modern" projects.' Similarly, although their legitimacy seems to stem from what he calls 'local forms of organisation,' in reality, they are largely dependent on the modern state. Geschiere concludes his study by arguing that while democratisation and multiparty politics have created an enabling environment for the return of 'old political actors', it is difficult to perceive them as a 'real alternative to State power' precisely because they seem to have become 'part of the State elite' (ibid. 169). Although he does not tell us whether chiefs have retained enough prestige to serve as 'vote banks' in the democratic era, the present study reveals that chiefs in the Grassfields of Cameroon have been unable to play this role.

There seems to be a striking parallel between developments in the North West Province of Cameroon and chieftaincy issues in Ghana. Boafo-Arthur (2001) contends that the Ghanaian Constitution clearly prohibits chiefs from participating in 'active' politics[12] but not necessarily in the democratic process. This has led to divisions among chiefs who are torn into two opposed camps. On the one hand, a number of chiefs maintain that the Constitution infringes on their civic and basic right by debarring them from playing an overt role in party politics. On the other hand, majority of the chiefs contend that 'a Chief who dabbles in politics is likely to be treated like a politician who could be hooted or booed. This would not only undermine his position but ultimately desecrate the institution of Chieftaincy as a whole.'[13] Boafo-Arthur argues that many prominent chiefs in Ghana are not respected because they are seen as 'allies of the ruling government.' He substantiates his case with the example of the *Osu Declaration*, passed by a number of prominent chiefs whose views were ignored because they were perceived by the people as 'willing tools of the government of the day.'

Jua (1995) arrives at a similar conclusion in his study of chiefs in the North West Province of Cameroon. He argues that the state does not only seek to undermine the institution of chief, but also to 'capture' it. This is evident in the legislation that defines and regulates the role of chiefs in postcolonial Cameroon. According to Jua, the state seeks to 'convert chiefs into clients' leading the relationship between the two to take on a 'semblance of parasitism rather than symbiosis...'(ibid. 43). From his observation of developments in Cameroon since 1990, Jua arrives at the conclusion that 'people could reject the authority of a chief who still commands the government's stamp of legitimacy' (Jua 1995:43). This conclusion has profound implications for the present study on chiefs and democracy in the Grassfields of Bamenda particularly with regard to the dynamics of how the relationship between chief and subject is shaped by the former's political choices.

In his study of 'chieftaincy in the modern state', Fisiy (1995) raises critical issues that also have implications for our understanding of chieftaincy in South Africa. He contends, much like Maloka, that the postcolonial terrain is a space contested by different political actors, old and new. According to him, chiefs also want to participate in 'inventing the future' of the postcolony. In order to understand their role properly, he argues, it is important to examine 'the relation between their control over people and over resources' the most important of which is land. For most rural people, he argues 'the control and management of land is at the heart of control over people' (ibid. 50). His research therefore focuses on the ways in which traditional leaders make use of their 'control and management of land' as a resource for power in the postcolonial state. By successfully creating a political space 'within which they can maintain their control over people and resources', chiefs are able to contest the postcolonial terrain and lay claim to local and regional power. Against this background, Fisiy poses an important question often ignored in many studies of chieftaincy and democracy, namely: does the discourse of democratisation as propounded in the African context, provide the most appropriate framework for inventing the future, given the pluralistic composition of African societies (ibid. 49)? It seems to me that a study of chiefs and democracy in South Africa and Cameroon should take this question into account as a guide to a deeper analysis of the predicament of chiefs in the current era.

Lastly, Nyamnjoh (2002c) argues in his study of chiefs and democracy in Cameroon that chiefs are agents whose political choices are contingent on their personal interests. Since the reintroduction of multiparty politics in Cameroon, he argues, chiefs have successfully made it to the forefront of national politics, sometimes in competition with other chiefs and chiefdoms. By actively and openly supporting the ruling Cameroon Peoples' Democratic Movement (CPDM), many chiefs in the grassfields of Cameroon have 'mobilised themselves under various lobbies to demand more recognition and resources from government.' He calls for an approach that recognises the 'agency of chiefs and chiefdoms as individuals and cultural communities seeking 'rights and might' as both 'citizens' and 'subjects' in the modern nation-state' (ibid. 8-14).

Much of the debate on chieftaincy has focussed on contemporary exigencies such as its interaction with the postcolonial state and, more recently, its predicament in the face of democratic reforms, and it has often failed to appreciate the relevance of the classical anthropological literature on chiefs in Africa. A reading of this literature provides deep insight into the past conditions of chieftaincy and how it has changed over the ages. I argue in this volume that a comprehensive analysis of the current situation of chiefs in the democratic era must take the classical literature into account, because it enables one to identify and understand the changes and continuities affecting chieftaincy. Here, I wish to examine very briefly, two of the classic studies by Max Gluckman (1940) and Isaac Schapera (1970).

In his 'Analysis of a Social Situation in Modern Zululand' Max Gluckman (1940) demonstrated the intercalary position of the Zulu Regent and his *indunas* (chiefs) in the face of increased European domination. The chiefs became part of the 'Governmental system' but still retained their 'traditional background' although they had 'little political influence in ... fundamental economic aspects of Zululand life' (ibid. 18). This could be buttressed by the fact that some educated Zulu Christians observed that the institution of chief was outmoded. They also described chiefs as reactionaries who opposed progress (Gluckman 1963). Nevertheless, Gluckman observed that the Zulu frequently compared Zulu officials and European officers and switched their allegiance according to what was to their own advantage. By showing their loyalty to the Zulu Regent for instance, the Zulu used an occasion such as the opening of the bridge to express their dissatisfaction with the colonial government.

Similarly, Schapera (1970) observed in his book *Tribal Innovators,* that Tswana chiefs were fast to adapt to changes brought to their chiefdoms as a result of the colonial encounter. Chiefs introduced innovations such as traffic regulations, taxation of several kinds and active support to the Europeans whom they admitted into their chiefdoms. Chiefs also encouraged their people to buy ploughs and other imported goods and to earn money for 'new wants' by going to work abroad in the mines at Kimberley. He notes further that such adaptation was not unique to Tswana chiefs granting that 'it has been known for over a century that chiefs in other groups of Southern Bantu sometimes also made social changes through legislation and in other ways' (ibid. 9). What we see in the two preceding paragraphs is that many of the issues affecting chiefs and chieftaincy today are not new. Since colonial times they have been intercalary figures, serving the modern projects of the colonial state as well as the 'traditional' aspects of their chiefdoms. We also see that, sometimes, chiefs were 'innovators' who were keen on 'modernising' their chiefdoms and introducing major changes. Later in this volume, I will show how this observation is true of Tshivhase in the post-apartheid era. The view that chiefs are reactionaries and opposed to change is in many respects not new. Gluckman shows that, as far back as the 1940s, some educated Zulu expressed this opinion. Thus, there seem to be a gap in much of the literature in the sense that it fails to reflect the continuities that date to colonial times. This volume will incorporate these issues in order to stimulate discussions that take into account the relevance of the past.

Given the above dynamics, I argue that exhortations to abolish chieftaincy in South Africa are clearly premature. Chiefs have not become outmoded by the introduction of democracy because they have yet again taken on a new role under the contradictory circumstances of neo-liberal democracy. The fact that the role is new is shown by the reality that not all chiefs of the previous era can participate with equal success. Chief Tshivhase is an example of how the new game is played successfully, at least until now. I also argue in the case of *fon* Ganyonga that although his overt association with the ruling party in the democratic era has tended to undermine his popularity at the local level, his relationship with his subjects is not completely ruined. This is because the contradictory nature of the democratic transition in Cameroon provided him the scope to join forces with other chiefs to articulate issues to the government on behalf of their people. Although Ganyonga's claim to legitimacy as a modern politician was contested by his subjects, he made attempts to legitimise his involvement in politics in the democratic era by throwing his weight behind the 'Anglophone cause' – at least during the 1990s.

[17]

This work is informed by the practice approach which, despite its many strands, generally seeks to explain the relationship(s) that exist between human action and the social system (Ortner 1984). I draw on the concept of *positioning* enunciated by (Holland and Leander 2004) which aims to explain the ways in which social agents position themselves in relation to the people, places and problems they encounter. This concept 'helps us recognize possibilities, albeit modest ones, of agency on the parts of the people who are the would-be subjects of positioning' (Holland and Leander 2004:130). Against this framework, this book argues that chiefs should be understood as social agents with the capacity to position themselves in varying contexts – first to prevail in the face of competing alternatives and secondly to legitimise their rule and political choices. Thus, the ethnographic evidence summoned in this book will show that the chiefs in Tshivhase and Bali are not only dynamic in matters of custom, but also how deeply involved they are in positioning themselves as representatives of the voices of their rural people – thereby seeking to legitimise their participation in modern politics in the democratic era. As social agents, it is apparent that they are endowed with abilities to negotiate, bargain and manoeuvre in local, regional and national politics (Barrett 1996:99). But the idea of individual agency could be misleading – often understood as central to the notion of the rights-bearing autonomous person. Here, we broaden our understanding of agency, embracing individual fulfilment as well as the ways in which this notion 'negotiates conviviality with collective interests which may include but are not limited to ... cultural dimensions' (Nyamnjoh 2002b:111). Thus, the actions of the chiefs in this study have moral and political consequences both for their individual positions and the communities they purport to represent. The notion of positioning does not see chiefs as imprisoned in 'a tête-à-tête with a mythical tradition' (Bayart 1989:29), but as agents involved in situations, which they can manipulate for their personal and communal gains. The above framework also informs the comparative dimension of this book in which I attempt to analyse and explain the status of chiefs in both countries and the nature of their democratic transitions based on the ability of the chiefs to position themselves in changing structures as they continue to seek new avenues for the relevance of "custom" and "tradition" in new political dispensations.

Research Method

This project is the outcome of a study conducted between May 2001 and March 2002 starting with research in the Tshivhase area of Venda, and culminating with fieldwork in Bali, Cameroon. A period of three months was devoted to each field site making use of qualitative methods involving unstructured interviews and extensive observation. Follow up field trips were made in 2005 and 2006 in Bali and Venda respectively.

Research in Venda commenced in May 2001 following an earlier trip in April to establish relevant networks and acquaint myself with the social and geographic setting. My research activities involved attending meetings at the chief's *khoro* (court) and the Territorial Council at Mukumbani (the capital of the Tshivhase territory), and visiting civic organisations in several satellite villages under Chief Tshivhase. People were interested in the study although initially, informants had difficulty in believing that I was not a MuVenda even though it soon became obvious that I could hardly understand or speak Tshivenda, and that my accent in English was demonstrably not South African. My identity as a young black African researching chieftaincy posed initial questions, but with time, people accepted the fact that I was a harmless outsider trying to make sense of chieftaincy in their area.

One thing I found interesting about the study in Venda was the reflexivity of the entire process. Most informants always turned the questions back to me - seeking to know if I had chiefs in my country and what their role was. They wanted to know if chiefs in my country were respected, married many wives and had magical powers. They also frequently asked if we had female chiefs in our villages, and how individuals acceded to chieftaincy. Doing research in Venda obliged me continuously to adopt a comparative perspective in understanding chieftaincy since inevitably, I was compelled to think of chiefs in Cameroon while observing the interactions of chiefs in Venda. I had interviews with chiefs and members of the royal families, commoners, members of the civic associations, the mayor and municipal councillors, and many of the youths as well as adult residents of rural areas. Because the villages under Tshivhase are numerous, I limited myself to four districts: Mukumbani, Vhufuli, Tshilapfene and Ngudza. Upon completion of fieldwork in Tshivhase, I left for Cameroon to pursue the second phase of the project. Despite having left Venda, I maintained communication with several key informants by regular phone conversations in order to catch up on gossip and developments. I also followed news about Venda via a website devoted to news coverage of the Limpopo province. In May 2002, I paid a short visit to Tshivhase to observe new developments, and collected data that I had overlooked during previous trips.

In Bali, entry into the field was made possible by the indirect assistance of an important title-holder of the chiefdom. Through him, I gained access to other elders and notables, especially the vice-president of the Bali Traditional Council, who had been charged with leadership functions in the absence of the chief. The advantage I had in Bali was my ability to understand and speak *Mungaka* (the language of the Bali Nyonga people) and *Pidgin* (the lingua franca in Cameroon). As in Venda, I made use of unstructured interviews, observation, and newspaper articles about developments in the chiefdom. My informants consisted of Bali residents (men and women), municipal councillors, notables (title-holders), traditional councillors, civil administrators and youths. I also visited local gatherings (*Ndakum*), which were held on Sundays, and picked up on local gossip.

In the end, a total of 80 interviews were recorded in Venda and Bali. I also devoted time to archival research. Since 1990 there has been a tremendous pool of newspaper articles devoted to discussions on chiefs and democratisation. Thus, archival data on the chiefs and the grassfields have been used to complement primary findings. Unless indicated otherwise, the names of my informants have been changed for the purpose of confidentiality.

Organisation of Book

This book consists of six chapters linked by the core themes of legitimacy, local and national politics and multiparty democracy. Two chapters are devoted to the

[19]

Tshivhase chiefdom in South Africa and two to Bali in Cameroon. A last chapter compares the trends and differences in both chiefdoms and the implications they have for our understanding of democracy and the postcolonial state in both countries. Theoretically, the book is informed by the practice approach of social positioning as articulated by Holland and Leander (2004). Positioning, they contend, should be seen broadly as part of a productive process in the course of which people, problems and places are culturally imagined and socially produced (Holland and Leander 2004: 130). As a matter of fact, the concept of positioning 'directs attention to how positions are produced in particular historical periods and to the social coordination necessary for successful positioning to be achieved, and it problematizes the subjective consequences of experiences of positioning for those who participate' (Holland and Leander 2004:130). This study will describe and explain the various positionings assumed by the chiefs under study, focusing in particular on the "problems", "places" and persons at the centre of the chiefs' lives and activities.

While some have argued and quite convincingly that chiefs have been corrupted by successive colonial, postcolonial and apartheid regimes and consequently should be excluded from local and national politics in the democratic era, there is strong evidence that chiefs remain and will continue to play influential roles in the lives of their subjects in rural and possibly in some urban areas across the continent. It should also be highlighted that chiefs are ambivalent figures, located between the state and their local communities and that chiefs do not necessarily contradict democracy nor do they enhance it, although they have the potential to serve as a bedrock on which democratic regimes can be built. I argue that invocations for the calculated marginalisation of chiefs from national and regional multiparty politics is premature and indeed disingenuous.

Chapter two is principally historical. It presents the historical background to the chiefdom of Tshivhase since the eighteenth century to the apartheid era. It describes the story of Venda migration to its present site, its 'glorious era' under Thohoyandou and its disintegration after his death. With the advent of colonial rule and later, the crystallisation of the apartheid state, Venda is reunified as a homeland under the leadership of Chief Patrick Mphephu who traces his descent to the legendary leader, Thohoyandou. Venda eventually becomes an independent homeland in 1979, still under Mphephu. The chapter ends with the increased demand for an end to the homeland and apartheid systems, the rise of Kennedy Tshivhase to power in the Tshivhase chiefdom and the re-incorporation of Venda into South Africa in 1994, following the demise of apartheid.

Chapter three poses and answers some of the sociological questions regarding the status of chiefs in Tshivhase. It examines the interaction between chiefs, subjects and the new democratic local government in Thohoyandou. Broadly, the chapter answers the key question: why in the democratic era has the chief become popular despite the presence of new democratic structures?

Chapter four presents a historical overview of the chiefdom of Bali in the North West Province of Cameroon. It examines in similar manner as in chapter two, the migration history of the Bali to their present site and the advent of colonial rule. This chapter shows the regional influence of successive Bali chiefs during the colonial period and in particular, the involvement of its legendary leader, Galega II in the struggle for the independence of the British Southern Cameroons. It also highlights the postcolonial episode and the policies that define the role of chiefs in local and national politics. The chapter ends with the rise to power of Ganyonga III in 1985 and the popular demand for democratic reforms that led to the re-introduction of multiparty politics in 1990.

Chapter five examines why fon Ganyonga III who had been a popular chief before 1990 became unpopular following the introduction of democracy in Cameroon. The chapter argues that although Ganyonga's legitimacy was initially undermined owing to his association with a self-serving party, he has nonetheless, won new legitimacy based on his dynamism and involvement in the so-called Anglophone problem. This chapter reveals the ways in which Ganyonga has coped with, and made use of the democratic era and why his leadership continues to find new scope despite his unpopularity in other spheres.

Chapter six is a comparative analysis of the status of both chiefs in their respective chiefdoms and countries. I draw on several theoretical approaches to interpret the differences and similarities that result from the ethnographic findings. I also show how my findings and interpretations relate to existing literature and on-going debate on chiefs and democracy in both countries. Lastly, I explore the implications of this study for our understanding of the democratic transitions in the two countries, and particularly the present character of the postcolonial state in South Africa and Cameroon.

Chapter Two
Rivalry, resistance and liberation politics in Venda

Introduction

This chapter deals with the historical background to the chiefdom of Tshivhase from the eighteenth century to the end of the apartheid era in 1994. It explores the migration history of the Venda to their present site, their so-called 'golden age' under Thohoyandou, and their subsequent disintegration into a multiplicity of small chiefdoms, of which Tshivhase is one. During the apartheid era, Venda was reunified as a homeland under the leadership of Chief Patrick Mphephu who traced his descent to the legendary leader, Thohoyandou. Venda eventually became an independent homeland in 1979, still under Mphephu's leadership. The collapse of apartheid in 1994 triggered an apparent reversion to old claims and renewed emphasis on the independence of each Venda chiefdom suggesting continuity in chiefdom rivalries despite the drastic change in contexts. Thus, this chapter seeks to show how chieftaincy and chiefdom politics in Venda can, in part, be seen as an on-going contest between the different chiefs and chiefdoms. The emergence of Kennedy Tshivhase at the helm of the Tshivhase chiefdom has clearly added nuance to the local rivalries.

A Political History of the Venda

While some historical accounts have maintained that the Venda (also called the BaVenda) came from the Congo region, others insist that they migrated from the Great Lakes of Central Africa over a thousand years ago and moved towards the southern part of Africa (BERCD 1979:17). Venda history is complex and the subject of unending dispute by different parties and dynastic groups that inhabit the territory. The scope of this study is not specifically historical and as such will limit itself to some of the secondary texts (both historical and anthropological) authored by ethnographers such as Stayt (1968) and Ralushai (1977; 1980).

Writing in the 1930s, Stayt argued that the Venda are 'a composite people' (Stayt 1968:9). Others have agreed with this view such as Loubser who contends that the Venda 'do not see themselves as a culturally homogeneous or politically united nation' (Loubser 1990:13; also see Ralushai 1977:46). Oral tradition suggests that most of the important migrations to the territory known today as Venda came from north of the Limpopo River in the 17th and 18th centuries. Among these migrations, two are particularly significant in the history of the area. The Vhatavhatsinde group arrived first, followed by the MaKhwinde from what is today known as southern Zimbabwe.[14] The latter is said to have found the Ngona group[15] 'a non-warlike rather disorganized people, who allowed the invaders to settle peacefully among them'[16] (Stayt 1968:10).

After the MaKhwinde migrated to Vendaland, led by their leader Dimbanyika, they soon dominated the entire country and settled at Tshieundeulu, where the Vhatavhatsinde had established their capital. Dimbanyika placed his sons and other kinsmen as petty chiefs throughout the villages and gradually incorporated the other groups under his leadership. Dimbanyika's reign did not last long as he died in c. 1720, after subjugating the other groups. Although the manner of his death is highly contentious among the Venda,[17] it is undisputed that his oldest son, Phophi, succeeded him and chose to call himself, Thoho-ya-ndou (Head of the Elephant) given that his father, the 'elephant,' had died. He then moved his capital to Dzata, which today is 'regarded as the ancestral home of the BaVenda' (Stayt 1968:12).

Stayt (1968) has described Thohoyandou's reign as the *golden age* of the BaVenda. This is because all the chiefdoms were united under his leadership. But after his death, internecine disputes precipitated the disintegration and division of the kingdom. Oral tradition holds that at the time of his death Dimbanyika had four adult sons of whom Phophi was the oldest. He had appointed them as petty chiefs in satellite villages: Phophi (Thohoyandou) ruled in Nzhelele, Tshisebe in Makonde, Tshivhase in Phiphidi, and Bele in Vuba. After Thohoyandou's death the other brothers declared their villages independent of the capital. Loubser (1990) estimates that this event may have taken place between 1750 and 1800. Although Thohoyandou's son, Tshikalanga was appointed to take over from his father, Venda was already disintegrating into several autonomous chiefdoms. This fragmentation was exacerbated by the advent of European invaders and colonialists.

Of the several lines of descent of Dimbanyika, the Mphephu and Tshivhase are the most numerous and powerful. The Mphephu leadership traces its descent from Tshikalanga and has established its capital at Nzhelele where Thohoyandou had ruled before becoming the King of the Venda. Other chiefdoms that were recognised by the colonial and apartheid authorities are the chiefdoms of Senthumele, Khuthama and Rambuda. The Mphaphuli area is the third most populated Venda territory, although its history is shrouded in a web of complexity that falls beyond the scope of this study (see Ralushai 1980 on the history of the Mphaphuli area).

This study is limited to discussions about the Tshivhase dynasty, which has dominated the eastern section of the Venda territory. After the death of his older brother Thohoyandou, Tshivhase declared himself independent. He became a wealthy and powerful chief and was succeeded by his son, Mukesi Tshivhase. Stayt (1968:16) contends that Mukesi's reign was marked by frequent skirmishes with his neighbours, especially Chief Mphaphuli, an independent chief living close to him. When Mukesi died, he was succeeded by his son Legegisa, who moved his capital from Miluwani to Mukumbani, the present Tshivhase capital. His son, Ramaremisa Tshivhase succeeded him and was in turn succeeded by Ratshimphi Tshivhase (circa 1931). Ratshimphi was a powerful and wealthy chief, who, to date, remains a legendary figure among the Tshivhase people. Local accounts hold that he resisted Boer encroachment into his territory so resolutely that it cost him his life. Some informants maintain that during his reign Ratshimphi joined the Communist Party in the 1930s, and was arrested by government forces for fear that he would turn his chiefdom into a communist stronghold. He was incarcerated in Pretoria where he died in 1946 and was succeeded by Thohoyandou Tshivhase, the father of the present chief, Kennedy Tshivhase (see genealogy of the Tshivhase dynasty – appendix 1).

Chiefs, Government and Politics in Venda (1913 – 1994)

Modern local government began in Venda in 1913, when the government of the Union of South Africa demarcated specific territories as 'reserves' for black people. The Native Affairs Act, 23 of 1920 provided for the establishment of local councils and a Native Commission to advise the South African government on issues that affected black people. The most significant legislation was the Bantu Authorities Act 68 of 1951, which provided for the creation of 'tribal', regional and territorial authorities. As a result of this Act, 25 tribal authorities, three regional authorities and one territorial authority were established in the Venda area (BERCD 1979:41).

Given its obsession with ethnic difference, the apartheid government emphasised that each ethnic group or people was endowed with the inalienable right to become self-governing in its own territory and to mark out the path of its own historical destiny. In the light of this ideology, the Venda were recognised not only as distinct from non-Venda, but also as a single people, or 'volk', which should commence the process of becoming an entity with its own territorial state. This led to the formation of the Thohoyandou Territorial Authority in 1962 headed by Chief Patrick Mphephu. According to this development, two or more members represented each of the 25 tribal authorities in a regional authority, one of whom was the chief or headman. The regional authorities were represented in the Territorial Authority by their chairmen and other members depending on population size and the number of taxpayers (BERCD 1979:42).

After the issuing of proclamation R.168 of 20 June 1969, the Thohoyandou Territorial Authority became known as the Venda Territorial Authority. This led to several changes in the form of representation. Each tribal authority was represented at the Territorial Authority by its chief or chairman and another member, elected by the tribal authority from among its councillors. The Territorial Authority was also granted more powers to conduct its own affairs with less direct control from the South African government. This development was further strengthened in June 1971 when the Black States Constitution Act No. 21 was passed. This Act provided for the creation of so-called Legislative Assemblies, one of which was constituted in Venda in February 1973, thereby making Venda a 'self-governing territory'. The legislative assembly was made up of 60 members, 42 of whom had to be traditional leaders. The remaining 18 were elected by the residents of Venda as well as Venda citizens who were resident outside Venda territory. Eventually in 1979 Venda received 'independence' from the Republic of South Africa but the international community refused to recognise this new status (BERCD 1979:42).

Of the 25 tribal authorities that make up Venda, Tshivhase is the most populated and largest in land area. This notwithstanding, there is an on-going contestation among the 25 tribal authorities (each of which constitutes a separate chiefdom), especially between the Mphephu and Tshivhase chiefdoms, which are, in genealogical terms, the 'senior' Venda chiefdoms. Although the Tshivhase still engage in some degree of rivalry with the neighbouring Mphaphuli chiefdom,[18] the relationship between the two is less contentious than that between Tshivhase and Mphephu.

One of the reasons for this rivalry is that the Tshivhase perceive the Mphephu as having been more accommodating to the colonisers than they were. This is a reference both to the Mphephu role in the wars against the Boers between 1867 and 1899[19] and to their collaboration with the apartheid regime. The Tshivhase also perceive the Mphephu group as more 'acculturated' owing to their geographical proximity to the white settlements of Louis Trichardt and Schoemansdal. In particular the Tshivhase resent the fact that Patrick Mphephu lorded it over their chiefdom in his attempt to revive the Venda kingdom during the homeland period. The last factor should be taken into account in order to understand current chiefdom politics in Venda. The Tshivhase continue to see themselves as the 'embodiment' of the fighting spirit of the Venda as expressed in their name - Tshivhase, meaning 'one who burned and conquered the houses of the others'(Heyden n.d.:12). The relative wealth and prestige of the Tshivhase chiefs also contributed significantly to this perception that the Tshivhase were the most powerful Venda chiefs. To add to this catalogue is the claim that the grandfather of the present chief was a staunch member of the Communist Party and had personally known Nelson Mandela in the 1940s prior to his death as a captive of the colonial state. The Tshivhase therefore claim a legacy of association with resistance and liberation, although some historians have disputed this.[20]

It is probable that the main obstacle to Mphephu's dream of extending his hegemony beyond his chiefdom was the reputation and power of the Tshivhase chiefs. It is therefore likely that the sudden death of Chief Thohoyandou Tshivhase in 1966 played in Mphephu's favour. Although Kennedy Tshivhase was installed in 1970 as heir to the throne of the Tshivhase, his uncle, John Tshivhase was put in place as regent until it was deemed appropriate for Kennedy Tshivhase to assume effective office.

Between 1970 and 1990, Kennedy Tshivhase stayed with his mother and attended school in Polokwane (formerly Pietersburg). While he was away from the chiefdom, major developments took place that changed the landscape of politics in Venda. The most important of these was the independence of Venda in 1979 under the leadership of Chief Patrick Mphephu. Mphephu was a shrewd politician who collaborated closely with the apartheid regime in Pretoria. His Venda National Party (VNP) dominated the political scene, leaving the Venda Independence People's Party (VIPP) in permanent opposition. During the 1980s, Patrick Mphephu co-opted almost all the major chiefs in the other dynasties including John Tshivhase, the Regent of the Tshivhase chiefdom. Chief Mphephu declared himself president for life of the Republic of Venda. It was popularly believed that he also nursed the ambition of reuniting the entire Venda territory as a kingdom under his leadership although he tended to favour the recruitment of his Mphephu subjects into the civil service and it was rumoured that people from other chiefdoms, especially the Tshivhase, were discriminated against. But such discrimination was concealed by the co-optation of influential members of the Tshivhase royal family into his government. One of them was Kennedy Tshivhase's uncle, A. A. Tshivhase, who was appointed to a key ministerial post in Mphephu's government. A. A. Tshivhase had opposed Kennedy's selection as heir to the throne of Tshivhase. By virtue of his influential post in the government, he became the dominant political figure in the Tshivhase family, choosing which direction the family was to follow. Informants recall that during election periods, the Tshivhase Tribal Authority, headed by John Tshivhase, used to campaign for the VNP. Following his death in

1989, Patrick Mphephu was succeeded as President of Venda by Ravele, a close kinsman and ally.

Ravele took over power at a time when there was increasing demand for an end to apartheid rule and the abandonment of the homelands. The rise of civic associations in villages, advocating an end to the homeland system, had enormous impact on the stability of the government in Venda. Between 1989 and 1990 witchcraft accusations and murders became the order of the day in Venda, and Ravele's failure to quell the murders or maintain peace triggered a general sense of anger. Furthermore, his failure to pay civil servants and his poor management of the government led to a military coup in 1990, led by Brigadier Gabriel Ramushwana.

Ramushwana was a controversial figure. Some informants described him as a 'two-edge sword'. On the one hand, he was believed to be an ANC-aligned leader. Although there was no definite proof of his affiliation to the ANC, the fact that he had been in exile was interpreted as an indication of his covert membership. On the other hand, he had been a soldier of the South African Defence Force (SADF), and was therefore connected to the apartheid regime. Given this background, he was viewed with ambiguity by both those who supported the ANC advocating change, and those who had vested interests in the homeland system and therefore preferred the status quo.

It appears that Kennedy Tshivhase made strategic use of this climate of political upheaval to stage his entry into the public sphere. It is recalled that he printed thousands of T-shirts, bearing his image surrounded by the colours of the ANC. This tactical appropriation of the ANC's colours was generally interpreted among the youth as an indication of his affiliation to the liberation movement and, consequently, his desire for change and the introduction of democratic government. It was also during this period, which saw the eclipse of A. A. Tshivhase's political fortunes, that supporters of Kennedy Tshivhase launched the battle to reclaim the leadership of the Tshivhase people.

In the early 1990s, the Tshivhase Royal Council was divided into two camps: those who supported Kennedy's right to the throne and those who ardently opposed it. Informants recall that under the influence of the notorious A. A. Tshivhase, the Regent and his close allies embarked on a campaign to distort history, and present Kennedy Tshivhase as an upstart who desired to usurp power from the elders through unorthodox means. A significant number of headmen opposed Kennedy Tshivhase's claim to the throne, especially those who owed their position to the apartheid system and the Venda government in particular.[21]

Meanwhile, although Kennedy Tshivhase did not publicly identify himself with the ANC, he was known among the youth and the civics as the legitimate heir to the throne and a comrade. Those who supported his return made strenuous efforts to spread the notion that Kennedy was simply reclaiming what was rightfully his. A photograph of the 1970 installation was available to prove that there had been no distortion of historical fact. When he eventually won the legal suit against his uncle and assumed office in 1993, popular conjecture about his political affiliation was confirmed. Both the military leader, Gabriel Ramushwana and the ANC stalwart, Walter Sisulu were conspicuously present at his installation in Mukumbani. Sisulu was given an opportunity to address the people. By 1993 it became clear that Chief Kennedy Tshivhase was an ANC member who had played his cards cleverly in the 1980s.

Contrary to expectations that he would seek to depose the headmen who had opposed his struggle for the throne, he called instead for peace and unity among the Tshivhase people. He also appealed to the divided Royal Council to bury the hatchet and unite to build a strong chiefdom. Though royal informants were reluctant to discuss with me how far the healing process had gone, it was rumoured during fieldwork that major differences continued to exist between competing camps of the royal family.

Kennedy Tshivhase also extended a hand of reconciliation to the Mphephu dynasty. Informants recall that Kennedy Tshivhase was quite friendly with Dimbanyika Mphephu, Patrick's successor as chief. This did not stop him launching a legal suit to reclaim a number of Tshivhase villages that had been incorporated into the Mphephu territory during Patrick Mpephu's presidency.[22] When Dimbanyika Mphephu died in a car accident in 1998, Chief Tshivhase participated actively at the funeral and delivered a speech. He disapproved of Dimbanyika's successor, and this has strained relations between the two major Venda dynasties once more.

Chiefs and Liberation Politics in Venda

The 'colonising structure' according to Mudimbe (1988) consisted not only in the domination of physical space, but also in the reformation of 'native' minds as well as the integration of local economic histories into the Western perspective. This was achieved through various means, one of which, to borrow from Mamdani (1996) was to co-opt chiefs into a system of decentralised despotism. Chiefs were therefore implicated in the colonising structure at different levels and in different contexts, as illustrated by Maloka (1995) and Mamdani (1996).

In Venda, it is likely that the colonisers chose the Mphephu dynasty not simply on the grounds of their pliancy (as the Tshivhase would want us to believe), but also because of their seniority, which was undisputed by the other descendants of Dimbayika. The apartheid context also envisaged a reunification of the entire Venda under the leadership of Mphephu, which helps to explain why he sought to control and manipulate events in the other chiefdoms, especially in Tshivhase. But in the course of this venture, he provoked the wrath of many subjects, especially those in Tshivhase, whom it was commonly believed were discriminated against in regard to recruitment into the civil service. Mphephu's co-optation of John Tshivhase and A. A. Tshivhase into his government permitted him to penetrate even deeper into the administration of the Tshivhase chiefdom, for instance by influencing the appointment of headmen who supported him and his party, the VNP. Consequently, a significant number of headmen in Tshivhase and other chiefdoms owed their position to the apartheid system and to Patrick Mphephu in particular. Most of these traditional rulers became unpopular not only because they had gotten into office through dubious means, but particularly because they were charged with the execution of unpopular policies. The chiefs also made use of their office to engage in various forms of 'primitive accumulation', which did not escape the notice of the subjects especially the youth.

Consequently, grievances against chiefs rose by the day. Chiefs in Venda were known to exact taxes and tributes of all kinds especially from migrant workers as a form of gratitude to the chief for looking after the migrants' families while they were away. Besides, migrants resented the law that compelled them to obtain permits from their chiefs before going to the city to work. When the pass laws were abolished in 1986, chiefs lost a major source of income and resorted to even more dubious forms of exploitation and exaction through the imposition of taxes. Reasons advanced for the imposition of new taxes ranged from the need to build new schools or clinics to the construction of post offices. Moreover, taxes were demanded to pay for the chief's legal advice where the chief or village was involved. Also, chiefs imposed taxes as contributions towards their marriages, the cost of royal funerals, and sometimes as payment for charges after consulting a rainmaker. If taxes were not demanded, free labour was imposed as a mode of exploitation. The usual victims were, more often than not, women and children. Free labour of this nature constituted working in the chief's *khoro* (chief's court) or on his farms, which most young women resented. Most men detested the chiefs because they could not hold any meetings without permission from them and were hardly consulted about decisions affecting their lives. Thus the assumption among migrants and other subjects that taxes benefited chiefs' private activities, not the good of the commonweal. Chiefs were accused of using tax money to build new houses for themselves or to buy new cars and repair old ones. Anger against the chiefs accumulated to such an extent that, by the 1980s, many rural dwellers seized the opportunity of UDF militancy to call for the overthrow of traditional institutions and chiefs.

In August 1983, the United Democratic Front (UDF) was formed to fill the institutional vacuum left by the African National Congress (ANC) and the Pan African Congress (PAC). The UDF provided a national 'political forum' for popular struggle amidst calls by the exiled ANC and South African Communist Party (SACP) for mass protest, formation of township organisations, ungovernability and the establishment of people's power (Houston 1999; van Kessel 2000). More precisely, the UDF was an 'alliance of a broad range of autonomous organisations of differing class origins and with differing political and ideological agendas which came together having identified a common cause - opposition to the apartheid system of domination and exploitation' (Houston 1999:5). Its primary aim was to mobilise existing movements throughout the country to participate in the liberation struggle. As a result, over 500 organisations were said to be affiliated to the UDF and united in 'unshakeable conviction' to dismantle the structures of apartheid and create a 'non-racial, unitary state in South Africa undiluted by racial or ethnic considerations as formulated in the bantustan policy' (Houston 1999:105).

Foremost among these affiliated organisations were civic associations of various kinds. Generally, civic associations mobilised and organised people around issues that affected their daily lives especially with regard to resources, rent and bus-fare increases. Many civic organisations emerged after the 1976 Soweto riots and grew in popularity thereafter (Houston 1999:105). In the townships, civic associations began to link local concerns with demands for the resignation of town councillors, the release of detainees and political prisoners, as well as the unbanning of political organisations.

News of these activities in urban areas diffused to rural areas and the homelands through the media, migrant workers, urban youths who attended local schools and boys who visited family and friends in the townships or who found temporary employment in the cities. Consequently, they carried news of their experiences as observers of or participants in the growing insurrection in townships and cities (Delius 1996).

Fed with the ideologies of prominent liberation fighters and the ANC, most youth 'set out to identify the forces of evil which were supposedly subverting their struggle' (van Kessel and Oomen 1997:565). The apartheid state also suffered both internal and external pressure to abandon its oppressive and discriminatory system and chiefs lost state support due to their inability to curtail rebellious youth and adults within their chiefdoms. For example, the abolition of the pass laws meant that chiefs could not punish rebellious subjects by withholding labour permits and travel documents. Chiefs were thus seen as a category ripe for eradication. In 1986 the UDF even alleged that democratically elected village councils were replacing tribal authorities and that it was only a matter of time for chieftaincy to be relegated to the annals of history (van Kessel 2000:75).

Ironically, young people arrogated to themselves the very chiefly powers they had purported to eradicate. Youths set up people's courts, beat up old men who failed to comply with their orders, and passed judgement on those they perceived and labelled as enemies of the 'struggle'. This insurrection also merged with witchcraft accusations and violence against many persons. Venda became the heart of witchcraft violence as a result of the revolt (Ralushai Commission 1996). A chief recounted the lamentable experience of being taken hostage by a band of violent youths and the horror of his colleagues who received death threats in the late 1980s. A number of chiefs were chased away from their villages and others sought refuge at the police station in Thohoyandou. In Tshivhase this violence was exacerbated by the inability of the unpopular acting regent, John Shavhane, to quell the unrest. Even police officers who were sent to several villages were reported to have failed to arrest any culprits, allegedly aimed at registering their contempt for John Shavhane.

However, the emergence of a chiefs' organisation which adopted the same rhetoric as the liberation fighters changed the tide of things for many chiefs in the homelands. The organisation first emerged as a result of several chiefs' fight against the scheduled 'independence' of the KwaNdebele homeland in 1986. In September 1987, the Congress of Traditional Leaders of South Africa (CONTRALESA) was launched with a membership of 38 chiefs and headmen mainly from KwaNdebele and the Moutse district of the Northern Transvaal. The new organisation had the lofty objective of uniting all traditional leaders in South Africa to fight for the abolition of the bantustan system, and among other things, to 'school the traditional leaders about the aims of the South African liberation struggle and their role in it.' It also spoke of winning back 'the land of our forefathers and share (sic) it among those who work it in order to banish famine and land hunger.' Above all, they pledged to fight for a unitary, non-racial, and democratic South Africa (South African Institute of Race Relations 1987-1988:922). News of its launch stirred a lot of shock and confusion among progressive circles who began to ask what they were going to do with chiefs who shared the same agenda as they did. CONTRALESA made strategic use of the rhetoric of *struggle* and advertised itself as a 'progressive grassroots and community based organisation.' This appeared contradictory given that chiefs were the ones who had opposed (and some were still opposing) the formation of civic associations, which were *par excellence* grassroots movements. This notwithstanding, chiefs reminded the people of the individual and

[29]

collective efforts of their forebears to keep colonialists at bay and to resist apartheid. Despite the initial suspicion, CONTRALESA gained legitimacy following the ANC's remarks that it was a sign of the 'chiefs coming back to the people' (Zuma 1990:65). It was as a result of this moral support and alliance with progressive forces that CONTRALESA was able to lobby its way into the talks towards a democratic South Africa.

After the ANC was unbanned in 1990, CONTRALESA's membership increased to over a thousand. Many chiefs saw the organisation as the best forum to safeguard their interest in a future ANC-led democratic government. Besides, the ANC was keen on co-opting traditional rulers in order to pre-empt alliances between the National Party (NP) and bantustan leaders. It should be noted that the Inkatha party of Buthelezi had very little popularity in Venda. Thus, chiefs were seen as occupying the middle ground between the ANC and the NP government. Their support could swing to either side (van Kessel and Oomen 1997:571-2). ANC's bid to win over the chiefs, though highly controversial in many circles, was seen as a major success.

Following the reintegration of Venda in 1994 into the Republic of South Africa, the tribal councils have continued to function as they did before, although their powers have been curtailed significantly by the Municipal Structures Act of 1993, as well as by recent legislation (see chapter three below). After the creation of the Thulamela Municipal Council (formerly Thohoyandou/Malamulele), 14 of the 25 tribal authorities (including Tshivhase) were integrated into the municipality while the others, including the Mphephu chiefdom, were incorporated in different municipal areas.[23] The Tshivhase Tribal Council has continued to play a major role in rural local government, more often than not, in serious conflict and rivalry with the new municipal authorities in Thohoyandou. The irony is that the mayor of the municipality is a headman under Chief Tshivhase.

The Tshivhase Tribal Council continues to function as the supreme judicial and administrative arm of government in the chiefdom. However, since the coming into office of Kennedy Tshivhase, there have been several changes in its organisation. At present, each village elects a delegate to accompany its chief to the grand meetings that are held four times a year. Once every five years, an executive council of the Tribal Council is elected composed of four chiefs and three commoners. A chairman runs the weekly activities of the council and reports regularly to Chief Tshivhase. The chief also has the discretion of appointing five additional persons to the executive council. But the most significant change is in its name. Formerly known as the Tshivhase Tribal Council, today it is officially called the 'Tshivhase Territorial Authority'. Although the reasons for this change are not obvious, it seems that Tshivhase has done this to emphasise the distinction and autonomy of his chiefdom from other Venda chiefdoms.

Furthermore there seems to be an on-going attempt by the ruling elite (led by Chief Tshivhase) to transform the chiefdom into a 'kingdom'. During fieldwork, minor chiefs and other commoners frequently referred to Chief Tshivhase as 'King' although the government has given recognition to no king in the Limpopo Province. In the light of these developments, some of his influential headmen are now known as 'chiefs.' The Tshivhase do not only speak with extreme pride about their numerical strength when compared to other Venda chiefdoms, but also about the number of villages that make up the chiefdom. Tshivhase has 74 villages and consequently 74 headmen. Thus, Chief

Tshivhase aims at building a powerful 'Territorial Authority' that could be recognised by the government as a kingdom. His claim to 'kingship' in Tshivhase, some informants observed, clearly excludes any claim over other Venda chiefdoms in contrast to Patrick Mphephu who is still resented for having used his dominant role in the homeland government to attempt a revival of the ancient Venda Kingdom.

Conclusion

The central objective of this chapter was to situate the chiefdom of Tshivhase in historical perspective and to show how the present dynamics in the chiefdom are a function of its interrelationship with other Venda chiefdoms since the 18th century. By means of historical analysis, I have argued that current trends in Tshivhase reveal substantial continuities despite changing contexts during the last 200 years. These contexts could be classified into three broad categories; the pre-colonial, colonial/apartheid and postcolonial era.

The pre-colonial era showed the migration of the different groups to the present area known as Venda and the eventual crystallisation of the Venda kingdom under the leadership of Dimbayika and later, Thohoyandou. During his reign, Thohoyandou was able to maintain a high degree of internal coherence, thereby uniting the several chiefdoms under his leadership. This unity was short-lived granting that the kingdom soon disintegrated into small autonomous chiefdoms following his death between 1750 and 1800. This fragmentation continued into the colonial era, which started in the late 19th century. Three chiefdoms emerged more powerful than the rest, that is the Mphephu, Tshivhase and Mphaphuli chiefdoms. Whereas the Mphephu chiefdom claimed direct descent from the legendary leader, Thohoyandou, the Tshivhase maintained that although their founder had been a brother of Thohoyandou, they owed their vast territory to their 'fighting spirit' and the relative wealth of their chiefs. These claims led to rivalry between the two senior chiefdoms which continue to date.

The colonial/apartheid era orchestrated a reconfiguration of chiefdom politics in Venda. This led to the reunification of the different chiefdoms under the leadership of the Mphephu dynasty, thereby defeating the efforts of the other chiefdoms to maintain their autonomy. Mphephu's collaboration with the apartheid regime favoured his dominance in homeland politics and his eventual emergence as the president of the 'independent' Republic of Venda. Although the apartheid era favoured the pre-eminence of Mphephu, his ambition to revive the old Venda Kingdom under his leadership (by means of manipulation and intrigue) instead triggered hostility towards his rule. The demise of the apartheid state and consequently the abolition of the homeland government led to the re-assertion of the autonomy of individual chiefdoms.

In the postcolonial context, the chief of Tshivhase has emerged as the new dominant figure. His emergence has been accompanied by the sidelining of the Mphephu chiefs by the post-apartheid state. The exclusion of the Mphephu chiefdom from the Thulamela Municipal area can be seen as a case in point. Nevertheless, while Chief Tshivhase has become involved in regional and national politics (as the late Mphephu was during the homeland period), the present chief of the Mphephu chiefdom has become less and less influential similar to the status of the regent of the Tshivhase during the apartheid era.

Given the above trends, we see that although the contexts have changed there is continuous contestation and rivalry among the Venda chiefs especially between the Mphephu and Tshivhase dynasties. We see from the historical trends that the main stuff of this rivalry has been the struggle between unification of several chiefdoms under one leader and the emphasis of each chiefdom's autonomy as a separate and independent entity. One can also deduce from the foregoing that in conditions of the above nature, new forms of inclusion invariably lead to exclusion. Whereas the Mphephu dynasty emerged as the dominant lineage during the apartheid era, the Tshivhase have emerged as dominant in the present democratic dispensation.

Be that as it may, it is imperative to return to some of the key questions posed in the introductory chapter; why has Chief Tshivhase used his position as a springboard into national politics? Why has he become involved in the political structure of the ruling party? Based on secondary sources and my own findings in the field, this chapter has answered the above questions by presenting in chronological order, the emergence of Chief Tshivhase at the helm of the Tshivhase chiefdom and his subsequent role in local and national politics. Among the evidence produced in the chapter, the following factors account notably for Tshivhase's rise and involvement in national politics.

First, he had the fortune of being a minor at his installation and as such did not have to grapple with the problems which he would otherwise have faced under Mphephu's presidency. The fact that he effectively assumed office towards the end of the homeland period means that he emerged untainted by the stigma associated with other chiefs in the Venda area who had participated in various ways to propagate the apartheid system. But fortune in itself is not enough to account for Chief Tshivhase's involvement in post-apartheid politics on the side of the ruling party.

He also associated himself with liberation fighters who were well known among the masses. This was evident during his re-installation in 1993 when the renowned ANC leader, Walter Sisulu was given an opportunity to address the masses. He was also close to Gabriel Ramushwana, the military leader who had overthrown Patrick Mphephu's handpicked successor as president. Thus, it is evident that Tshivhase had laid the groundwork for his eventual rise into the ranks of the ANC and, consequently, national politics.

It should also be borne in mind that hereditary elites tend to benefit or suffer from the actions of their forebears. In this particular instance, there is evidence that Tshivhase benefited from the legacy of his legendary grandfather, Ratsimphi who had been involved in the Communist Party in the 1930s and, through such association, had known Nelson Mandela. Tshivhase claims that Nelson Mandela still has fond memories about his grandfather not only because of his resistance against the 'Boers' but also for his involvement in the liberation struggle in the ranks of the Communist Party. Kennedy Tshivhase could be seen as taking over from the legacy of his grandfather and therefore deriving legitimacy of some kind in this respect.

Last, the chapter has shown that the ANC sought to co-opt chiefs in general and 'progressive chiefs' in particular into its ranks in order to pre-empt possible alliances between the chiefs and the NP. It was precisely against this background that few chiefs such as Kennedy Tshivhase quickly gained prominence and prestige in the ANC, and therefore his involvement in national politics. Clearly, a combination of the above

[32]

points accounts for Tshivhase's popularity not only at the local level but also at the provincial and national levels.

This chapter has also examined the unpopularity of the homeland system in Venda, and the chiefs who were at the helm of this system. This generated hostility towards chiefs in general and certain prominent chiefs in particular such as Chief Mphephu. It was against this background that many civic activists anticipated the demise of chiefs in the post-apartheid era. However, the introduction of democratic rule ushered in new contradictions, which again, have permitted chiefs to play a "new" role. But the reality is that not all chiefs have the legitimacy to play this role in the neo-liberal context. In the next chapter I will show what changes have resulted from the introduction of democratic rule and the new role played by Chief Tshivhase in this process.

Chapter Three
Chiefs, local government and social change in post-apartheid Tshivhase

We are not fighting with the government. We only want to help our government with the issues affecting us as Chiefs which is part of the African Renaissance.[24]

These efforts are part of our vision of the African Renaissance, to construct a progressive African state with a democratic form that is indigenous to our land and our continent. We will therefore spare no effort to ensure that in the deracialising and democratisation of local government, we take traditional leaders along with us.[25]

Introduction

In the preceding chapter, I examined the role and predicament of chiefs in Venda during the pre-colonial, colonial and apartheid era. This provided the reader with the historical background to the transformations that chiefs and the masses in Venda experienced until 1994. In this chapter, I will explore the changes that have taken place in Venda since 1994, particularly in the Tshivhase area where fieldwork for this study was carried out. In this respect, the following specific questions are raised and examined in detail: What has changed since the collapse of apartheid? What has brought about the changes? Who are the 'new' political actors? Who claims what legitimacy in the post-apartheid era, who is persuaded and why?

In order to answer the above questions, the chapter is divided into three broad sections. First, I examine some of the important policies that have dealt with the role of chiefs in the new democratic dispensation. It is crucial to understand the prevailing policy frameworks because it helps one to appreciate the processes taking place on the ground. Next, I consider the changes that have taken place in the past decade since the introduction of democratic local government and how the different political actors have interpreted these changes. I also address the various claims for legitimacy by different political actors specifically among traditional leaders and the democratically elected local council in Thohoyandou. The last section deals with the relationship between traditional leaders in Tshivhase and their subjects and the issues that have shaped this relationship – thus accounting for the greater visibility and popularity of some traditional leaders in Tshivhase.

Chiefs and Policy Framework in Postcolonial South Africa

Let me begin with the policy framework that informs chieftaincy issues in South Africa and how these have shaped the relationship between chiefs and the post-apartheid state, particularly with respect to local government. The general assumption is that the post-apartheid state has sidelined traditional leaders from national politics despite the fact that chiefs anticipated a more substantial role for themselves in the post-apartheid context. This view brings back into focus the predictions about the incompatibility of chiefs and democracy and the assumption that current legislation in

[34]

South Africa tends to advocate this (cf. Maloka 1996). One of the reasons for this so-called 'marginalisation' is the assumption that the ANC's good performance in past elections and its consolidation of power mean it is 'more confident that it could win on its own without cumbersome alliances with traditional leaders' (van Kessel and Oomen 1997:584).

My analyses point to two specific categories of legislation that deal with chiefs. These are on the one hand, those that focus on the role of traditional leaders vis à vis the postcolonial state and on the other hand those that address the relationship between chiefs and local government. In this connection there is some consensus that the 1993 interim Constitution was friendlier to chiefs than the 1996 Constitution. This 'friendliness' is attributed to the influential role that CONTRALESA played at the Convention for a Democratic South Africa (CODESA) talks and eventually the drawing up of the interim constitution. The 1993 interim Constitution for instance recognised the important role that chiefs could play in the nation-building project of the post-apartheid era and provided for the formation of Houses of Chiefs. Section 183 provided for the establishment of provincial Houses of Traditional Leaders with the functions of advising provincial legislatures on matters dealing with Traditional Authorities, indigenous law and the customs and traditions of traditional communities. Furthermore, Section 184 of the 1993 Constitution talked of the establishment of a Council of Traditional Leaders with the role of advising national government on matters pertaining to Traditional Authorities, indigenous law and the customs and traditions of ethnic communities.

By December 1996, four provinces had successfully established their own Houses of Chiefs although the Eastern Cape had difficulties establishing its House due to conflicts between chiefs and the civics (van Kessel and Oomen 1997:574; Maloka 1995:35; cf. Bank and Southall 1996). Similarly, the Limpopo Province was deadlocked in debate on basic issues about representation in the House. This is because the Limpopo Province has over 300 chiefs, with a majority of them coming from the former Lebowa homeland. There was a debate over what form of representation best suited the numerous chiefs from the former homelands in the province.

In regard to policies concerning chiefs and the state, the National House of Traditional Leaders was eventually established and launched on 18 April 1997 in Parliament following the National House of Traditional Leaders Act of 1997. According to this Act, the National House is expected to 'promote the role of traditional leadership within a democratic constitutional dispensation'. But critics of this legislation have pointed out that neither the Act nor the 1996 Constitution places an obligation on Parliament to refer any legislation to the National House (Du Plessis and Scheepers 1999:16).

The second set of policies pertaining to chieftaincy issues in the new South Africa deals with the relations between democratic local government and traditional authorities. These policies date back to 1993 and even earlier when most of the apartheid laws were repealed and discussions towards a democratic South Africa begun. The Local Government Transition Act No 209 of 1993 ironically excluded chiefs from effective participation in local government. This Act betrayed the advances that the interim Constitution had made to traditional leaders regarding their role in the postcolonial context. Actually, the Act considered chiefs simply as stakeholders (special interest groups), the same as farm owners, farm workers, women, civic associations and any other parties interested in democratic local government (cf. Ntsebeza 1998). Chiefs were clearly angered by this legislation and until today, still perceive themselves as betrayed by the ruling ANC.

This explains why CONTRALESA called for the boycott of the local government election scheduled for November 1995. Chiefs threatened that they would not only boycott the election but would also prevent it from being held in rural communities until the government was ready to reform the Local Government Act of 1993 and redefine the role of traditional rulers in local government. The ANC perceived these threats by chiefs as unjustified. It also interpreted this move by chiefs as an obstacle to the consolidation of its democratic gains.[26] Eventually, however, the election took place without any major incidents. The outcome was the establishment of Transitional Local Councils (TLCs) throughout the country. Although the 1993 legislation emphasised that the jurisdiction of TLCs would include the territories ruled by Tribal Authorities, it was acknowledged that effective governance of such territories would have to be a gradual process.

Soon after the democratisation of local government had begun, the final Constitution was enacted in 1996. Many chiefs talk of the Constitution with much contempt, for several reasons. First, the section devoted to chiefs (Chapter 12) is the shortest part in the Constitution. Such brevity, chiefs contend, is a demonstration of the government's nonchalance towards them. Chapter 12 of the Constitution also emphasises that the role of chiefs is restricted to 'custom' and 'tradition', although it fails to define what precisely it means by these terms. Finally, the Constitution maintains that future legislation on chiefs shall be provided by provincial and national government. Since then, however, not much has been done to address the role of chiefs except in the *White Paper on Local Government*. The government's draft *White Paper on Traditional Leaders and Institutions*[27] has not found favour with many headmen under Tshivhase who insist that the government has done little to accommodate the institution of chief in the current dispensation.

The *White Paper on Local Government* published in 1998 by the Department of Provincial and Local Government, endeavoured to address a few issues regarding the role of chiefs in local government. The policy document recognised the fact that there are huge tensions between Tribal Authorities and the new local councils owing to the fact that most of the functions that have been assigned to the new municipal authorities tend to overlap with those performed by the chiefs during the apartheid period. It is against this background that chiefs perceive the new municipal authorities not as partners or collaborators, but as rivals and usurpers. Although this may be the case, the *White Paper on Local Government* has identified three specific functions that chiefs perform and which do not conflict with those performed by the new municipal authorities. These functions are:

- Acting as head of the traditional authority, and as such exercising limited legislative powers and certain executive and administrative powers.
- Presiding over customary courts and maintaining law and order.
- Consulting with traditional communities through *imbizo/lekgotla* - grand tribal meeting to which all male adult citizens are invited.

Critics of the *White Paper on Local Government* have pointed out that the document does not make any provisions that include traditional rulers in discussions towards the establishment of boundaries between municipal council areas and tribal territories.[28] This omission has led to a degree of arbitrariness regarding the nature of boundary setting between tribal land (communal space) and municipal territories (private space). Later in this chapter I will show how this arbitrariness was played out in Tshivhase, and the sort of conflicts that have arisen in consequence.

Despite the above shortcoming, the *White Paper on Local Government* proposes a co-operative model of rural local government in accordance with the South African Constitution of 1996. The White Paper 'proposes that elected local government in areas falling under traditional leadership be constituted in such a manner that traditional leaders will be represented and have a role to play. Their role will include attending and participating in the meetings of the municipal councils and advising them on the needs and interests of their communities.' This is similar to the 'mixed government' approach advocated by Sklar (1986), the prospects of which were considered in the South African context by Bank & Southall (1996). Mixed government according to Bank and Southall refers to 'co-operative interaction among distinct and relatively autonomous governmental institutions' (ibid. 407). Given the prevailing socio-economic circumstances in most rural areas and the disaffection that chiefs have for the new municipal authorities, it is worthy to ask if 'mixed government' in Tshivhase is in any real existence.

Having examined the evolution of national policy on chiefs since the collapse of the apartheid regime, this chapter will proceed by exploring how these policies affected chiefs and their rural communities. To this end, the specific case of Tshivhase will be examined in detail.

Following the local council election of 1995, in which the ANC registered a massive victory in the Limpopo Province, an ANC-controlled Transitional Local Council (TLC) was established in Sibasa (later transferred to Thohoyandou). The TLC was charged with the overall administration and development of its municipal areas. This entailed *inter alia*, the delivery of services and the maintenance of roads. The advent of democratic local government was perceived as a welcome solution by all and sundry especially the rural people who had been excluded from council services during the homeland period. The democratisation of local government therefore was also interpreted as a democratisation of citizenship for all South Africans. It was in this light that the newly established TLC was extremely popular among urban and rural populations, even though the chiefs saw them as rivals.

A Municipal Demarcation Board was also established at the same time as the TLC. This Board was charged with drawing up new boundaries between tribal and municipal lands. The Board was also charged with the demarcation of 'stands' in urban and rural areas although chiefs strongly opposed what they perceived as the Board's encroachment into tribal lands. This became evident when the TLC and the Demarcation Board began 'interfering' with the administration of land in rural areas. Many of the new council members assumed that chiefs had no role in the new democratic dispensation and therefore saw it as incumbent on themselves to take over the management of rural affairs especially in matters of land. It is important to point out that this assumption among the new council authorities was not completely unfounded given the local government policy of the era, which perceived traditional leaders simply as a special interest group, similar to civics and property owners. Chief Tshivhase observed on this issue as follows:

> The Transitional Local Council did not understand [democracy] because they thought their goal was to replace chieftaincy in our area. That is why we had to sit down and discuss the matter by stressing that the government did not have the intention of doing away with chieftaincy, but that we must work together. (Chief Tshivhase, 21 May 2001)

When I talked to the Executive Mayor of the Vhembe District Council[29] based in Thohoyandou, he revealed that the prevailing assumption was completely in consonance with the spirit of that era. He contends that a wave of unprecedented euphoria characterised the advent of democratic local government, and that the TLC and rural civic associations believed strongly that it was the most appropriate time to replace chiefs and chieftaincy with 'peoples' power'.

> First of all, the chiefs had the impression that the transitional local government was eroding their powers. They noticed that the TLC was taking away their powers and consequently they would be left to live like ordinary people without any authority. This also meant losing their salary, which was their main source of livelihood, but my impression was that the TLC's approach was premature. They didn't have the information; they didn't even know the direction to which transitional local government was going. There was a lot of ignorance on the part of the councillors and officials.... In our situation for example, municipalities were new institutions amongst black people because they didn't know them. Previously, we had the traditional authorities, which were governing the rural people, so after the 1994 election, everybody was excited, everybody had power, everybody wanted to impress everybody else that 'away with apartheid and the chiefs'. The chiefs were stigmatised as collaborators of the apartheid regime, hence, they were undermined since the councillors thought this was a time to revenge, to take over the institutions from the previous authorities. (Executive Mayor, Vhembe District Council, 16 July 2001).

We see from the above that while the TLC was very popular with most rural dwellers and civic associations, traditional authorities rightly felt threatened by the new councillors. Another key informant, the Chairman of the Tshivhase Territorial Authority expressed the anxiety of the chiefs in the following way:

> They [municipal council] are the ones who want to take away our functions, but we have said no. They rather prefer that we should remain with those customs and rituals but we wouldn't accept that. If they take those functions from us, what are we going to do with the community, with the people under our rule? The people listen to us and whatever we are doing, they understand us better than those elected by the people. (Chairman of the Tshivhase Territorial Authority, 25 May 2001).

[38]

As much as the ideas of local government and service delivery sounded very appealing and lofty to the rural masses, it soon became obvious that delivery could be provided only to those who could afford and were willing to pay for the services. This 'obvious truth' belied the expectations of many rural dwellers who anticipated that the advent of freedom and democracy would entail the free availability of services. It was against this background that many rural dwellers became disillusioned when the TLC set the monthly delivery charge at R12 per person. The contradiction in this case was that the TLC introduced the 'rates' with the intention of raising money for services, but no services had been delivered. In other words, people were expected to pay for services they had not consumed. The fact that the TLC wanted to raise money in order to deliver services at a later period raised many questions among the rural populations who felt they might wait for a very long time (if not indefinitely) before enjoying the services they had paid for. Thus, municipal council authorities were accused of corruption informed by experiences from other Venda chiefdoms where rates had been paid without any service delivery in return. Furthermore the civic members were angered by the fact that the TLC did not consult with them before arriving at the price of R12.

Many people were also displeased by the fact that the local government was charging exorbitant fees in order to demarcate land for the rural masses. These developments resulted in the local council losing its claim to legitimacy in the eyes of the rural people, particularly among the civics who had hailed the introduction of democratic local government as a welcome alternative to chiefs. This contest offered space for some chiefs to make new claims for legitimacy by exploiting the weaknesses of the local council. Not all chiefs have been successful in this respect because some of them remain tainted by their past involvement in the structures of apartheid. Among those that have gained prominence is Chief Tshivhase whose experiences provide an example of the way in which the new game is played in the neo-liberal context.

Chief Tshivhase and Democratic Change

Chief Tshivhase makes two principal claims for legitimacy in the new dispensation. First he claims to be the rightful heir to the throne of the Tshivhase chiefdom, and second, he asserts that he is a protector of the rural poor against the market forces propagated by the local council. Although both claims resonate with a large proportion of the rural population, I will dwell on the second which deals with the substantive issue of socio-economic uncertainty in post-apartheid Venda. In this respect, Chief Tshivhase has successfully straddled his positions as both traditional ruler and ANC politician in order to enhance his prominence at both the regional and national levels. He has achieved this through various means, although I will limit the discussion to three key areas.

The first is that as an innovator, Chief Tshivhase made use of the Tshivhase Territorial Council to extend his legitimacy to the other chiefs under him and to counter the policies of the local government. Second, he introduced the Tshivhase Development Trust as an alternative arm of development in the chiefdom thereby assimilating and propagating the official discourse of 'development', which is prominent in ruling ANC circles (see White Paper on Local Government 1998). Last, he co-opted civic organisations in his chiefdom and harmonised the relationship between traditional rulers and these new forces along the lines of 'peoples' power'. This could be perceived as a means of ensuring a support base for himself among rural dwellers, including civic members, in and around his chiefdom.

I will expand on the above issues, first by exploring the changes he introduced through the Tshivhase Territorial Council (hereafter referred to as the TTC). Two issues should be borne in mind; namely that some of the changes were in direct response to the actions of the local councils and second, that some of these changes resulted from Chief Tshivhase's personal dynamism – the product of social positioning in changing socio-political contexts.

I effectively began fieldwork in May 2001 and still recall with much vividness, my first day at the TTC. The TTC held its meetings every Thursday morning at the headquarters in Mukumbani. On my first day of attendance at its deliberations, I was welcomed by the chairman and allocated a seat among the councillors. The meeting officially began with prayers led by one of the councillors. This was immediately followed by a session devoted to administrative matters, which involved scrutinising and deciding on various applications while the applicants waited outside. Over a dozen applications consisting of all sorts of requests were attended to. After the councillors had deliberated, the applicants were summoned into the council hall to receive their verdict. Mrs M was given permission to open a Spaza shop, Mr S was permitted to occupy a piece of land, Mr K was allowed to run an initiation school in the coming winter and so forth. But Mr P's application was turned down. Mr P was the principal of a local secondary school and had applied for permission to install pipe-borne water in his school. He was blamed for having ignored the due process of application by not going to his headman, in the first instance, before approaching the TTC. I found Mr P's case particularly interesting because it raised several issues regarding the control of land and access to basic resources. He was eventually asked to take his application back to the headman in whose village the secondary school was located. After the session described above, the councillors immediately moved to the next, which was concerned with judicial matters. Councillors used this period to listen to and solve important disputes that could not be resolved at the village level. The session lasted until late in the afternoon, after which business was officially concluded with a prayer from one of the councillors.

I have described in the preceding chapter how Chief Tshivhase changed the name of this institution from the Tshivhase Tribal Council to the Tshivhase Territorial Authority. Before this and other changes took place, the Tribal Council had become rather weak and helpless as a result of on-going scuffles among members of the royal family and the unpopularity of the regent. Even after 1994 the reformed council did not enjoy much legitimacy among the people. This explains why civic members still arrogated to themselves the powers of the chiefs to allocate and demarcate land in some villages and to run peoples' courts. But this did not last long given the developments that took place later, such as the introduction of the TLC. While the civics gradually retreated from competing with traditional authorities for reasons that will be explored later, the TLC began to make new claims of jurisdiction over tribal land. Although the TLC succeeded in other chiefdoms such as in the neighbouring Mphaphuli chiefdom, the Tshivhase chiefs succeeded in resisting what they perceived as an encroachment into their territory. Many informants observed that if chiefs lose their control over communal land, they risk losing their authority completely in the present democratic context:

> The land belongs to the king and the people and he has no title over the land. This is the base also for the legitimacy of the king. ... The subject is given the land freely and he has to till that land for as long as he is loyal to the king or the chief. The subjects have rights of tillage, grazing, gathering, right to residence, right to burial. As long as you are loyal to the king, you will be given land freely with all the above rights. (Mr. S, Member of Territorial Council).

The above quote is relevant for appreciating some of the changes introduced by Chief Tshivhase intended to tighten traditional authorities' grip over communal land. These changes were twofold. On the one hand, the TTC reduced the fee that subjects had to pay in order to be allocated land. While the fee varied from village to village, it was normally not more than R50 for a home stand. This amount was low when compared to that charged by the municipal council and to what chiefs in other chiefdoms charged their subjects. In the Mphaphuli area, for instance, people paid between R80 and R300 to procure a stand. In addition, people in the Mphaphuli chiefdom were also subject to the service charges meted out to urban residents, principally because their chief had not succeeded in standing up to the policies of the local council.

The second major change in Tshivhase dealt with the demarcation of land. While the municipal council charged a heavy sum for this process, the TTC decided to perform the same service for free. In addition to these changes, the TTC scrapped certain fees paid by subjects during the homeland era, such as fees to bury their deceased in the public cemetery, to gather firewood and to grow crops on small portions of land. These innovations can be illustrated with an example from one of the Tshivhase villages.

Victor was a civic member in the Tshivhase village of Mukula. He operated a small provision store in the village and business was doing very well. In February 2001 he realised he had made considerable profit, enough to expand his business as suggested by the growing demand for liquor in the village. So he resolved to build a small shop for the provision of liquor. After securing the approval of his headman, he took his case to the TTC and was granted the permission to extend his stand. In the same month, the TTC re-demarcated Victor's boundaries and updated his documents to that effect. As it had become customary for the TTC, a copy of the decision was sent to the municipal authorities and the Demarcation Board at Thohoyandou. Unexpectedly, the Demarcation Board queried the TTC's decision and accused it of interfering in the Demarcation Board's jurisdiction. The Demarcation Board proceeded to annul Victor's deed of occupation and requested that he should pay the sum of R3000 in order for the board to grant him an official title deed. But the TTC stood firm on its decision and directed Victor to carry on with his business, which he did without further intervention from the council authorities.

This brings me back to an important issue, namely the municipal council's provision of services at a market price. In Thohoyandou, there is a popular discourse about the privatisation of land and the need to democratise access to municipal services such as water, road maintenance and garbage disposal, but these services come at a price. Clearly, these issues are not new. Informants observed that this process began during the period of the TLC. The Executive Mayor of the Vhembe District Council for instance contended that the TLC attempted to provide services in rural areas only because it had run out of revenue. The authorities decided to set the so-called service charge of R12 with the intention of raising enough capital to sponsor some of its urban-based projects.

But things did not work out in the way they had anticipated. In Tshivhase for instance, Chief Tshivhase and his Territorial Council launched a campaign against the TLC and accused the council authorities of trying to dupe rural people. Informants recalled that the chairman of the TTC and other key councillors went to the Phalaphala FM radio in Thohoyandou where they called on subjects not to make payments of R12 as requested by the TLC. The people quickly heeded to their chiefs' call for several reasons. One of these was that the TLC had not delivered any services to rural dwellers. Besides, rural people did not want the municipal authorities to dispose of their garbage since they could and wanted to take care of it themselves. Some civic members insisted that the TLC had not negotiated the fee but had simply imposed it on them. Lastly, informants pointed out that given the high levels of unemployment in rural areas, the fee was simply unaffordable by most people.

When the new council authorities took over from the TLC following the council elections of December 2000, the fee was maintained although they admitted to me that no services had been delivered in Tshivhase due to the refusal of the chiefs to co-operate. The irony behind this is that the new mayor of the Thulamela council is a headman under Chief Tshivhase. Although he has made fewer claims than the former mayor, in terms of jurisdiction over tribal land, he still maintains that the R12 service charge should be maintained as a source of funds for future service provision. It is also common knowledge that he has a long-standing rivalry with Chief Tshivhase who is not only his senior in traditional government, but also in the ANC. Chief Tshivhase has threatened several times to suspend the mayor from his 'headmanship' but it is unlikely he will put his threats into action.

Many informants accused the municipal council of trying to exploit them and suggested that they would avoid the municipal council for as long as they could. Rural dwellers could not understand why the municipal authorities insisted on treating them in the same way as urban-based residents. According to them, villages are not suburbs, 'locations' or townships where the municipality is obliged to deliver services. What they needed, informants insisted, were jobs, not services.

The evidence above demonstrates that some of the changes introduced in the TTC resulted from the unpopular actions of the municipal council. Although it appeared as if Chief Tshivhase and his colleagues had been sidelined from the activities of the municipal council (given that they had no representation in the council board), the reality was that the chiefs had taken a stand against council authorities by emphasising the spatial and political demarcation between tribal territory and the municipality.

Other changes in Tshivhase were due to Chief Tshivhase's own personal initiative, cognizant of the fact that he was endowed with the unique status of positioning himself strategically in the defence of the rural poor and women in particular. For instance it was common knowledge that in the past era, women could not apply for plots of land except by proxy. This could be done only through an uncle, a father or a husband. Chief Tshivhase changed this discriminatory practice by granting women the same rights to land as men. According to him, this innovation was wholly in harmony with the South African Constitution, which provided for a non-sexist and non-racial South Africa. Chief Tshivhase supported his decision by pointing out that the Tshivhase chiefdom had female chiefs who played as important a role in tribal government as their male counterparts. Although some male informants expressed mixed feelings about this innovation, they admitted that the Chief had the interests of all subjects at heart regardless of their sex.

Chief Tshivhase also claimed legitimacy by virtue of his involvement in 'development'.[30] Besides his influential role as the executive head of the TTC, he was also a founding member of the Tshivhase Development Trust of which his cousin, a Johannesburg-based businessman was the CEO. The Trust's primary objective was to lobby funds and initiate development projects in the chiefdom and other Venda territories such as the construction of schools and the provision of small-scale employment opportunities. The Trust had a large plantation of timber and it recently acquired farms formerly owned by the defunct Venda Development Corporation (VDC). Chief Tshivhase claimed he had succeeded in providing employment opportunities for a few young people in his chiefdom by hiring them to work on the farms and plantations.

In 2001 the Trust registered two major success stories. First, it reached an agreement with New Africa Investment Limited (NAIL), a Johannesburg-based organisation, to provide school buildings covering approximately 3500m^2 of its territory. According to the agreement, the Limpopo Province Department of Education was going to own and maintain the buildings while the Trust would manage the sum of R4.8 million to undertake structural improvements and make additions to the Tshivhase High School. The Trust also made financial contributions for the construction and launch of a Community Library in the village of Ngwenani ya Mapholi in September 2001.

Another event that caused much sensation was Chief Tshivhase's visit to Germany in August 2001. This was not his first trip to Germany for business. He had made several trips before with a close German friend who grew up in Venda and was considered a subject[31]. What was different this time was the fact that six young individuals accompanied him. Their mission was to enable the six young subjects to acquire skills in Germany during a period of one month. Upon their return, it was anticipated that these individuals would share their skills with their peers in the chiefdom and possibly, enable them to become self-employed. During their one-month stay in Germany, three of the young persons obtained training in the art of metal design while the others had training in hotel catering and tourism.

Although this event could be dismissed as trivial from the point of view of its contribution to development, its significance was promoted by the TTC and the Tshivhase Royal Council, which organised a huge function to celebrate Chief Tshivhase's achievements in this respect. The event, which took place on 8 September 2001 at Mukumbani, was attended by leading politicians in the Limpopo Province, ambassadors from Pretoria and local elites. Other prominent Venda chiefs such as the

Mphaphuli were present although the Mphephu failed to show up. Chief Tshivhase used the opportunity to appeal to his fellow traditional rulers to join him in developing Venda. He also requested support (development aid) from foreign governments (represented by the ambassadors present) in order to extend the efforts of the Tshivhase Development Trust beyond the Tshivhase chiefdom. The spokesperson for the Trust, a Pretoria-based civil servant, further revealed that the Trust has begun negotiations to assist in development projects in other Venda chiefdoms.

Given the above trend, it could be asked if Chief Tshivhase has enough resources to carry out his ambitious plans for development. The reality is that even if he had substantial resources, he would be unable to meet the increasing demand for jobs in his chiefdom. Nevertheless, Chief Tshivhase has succeeded to provide for his people what some other chiefs have not been able to do – a shield against the scourge of the market forces, into which the local council desperately wants to draw them. In the next session I will examine the particular relationship between chiefs in Tshivhase and civic organisations which, as indicated above, posed a major threat to chiefly power in rural areas in the 1980s. This also permits the reader to appreciate the extent to which Chief Tshivhase has successfully extended his legitimacy to the headmen under him, despite the fact that some of them are apartheid-era appointees.

Traditional Leaders and Civics in the Democratic Era

'The closer we come to the political grassroots the closer we have to consider such 'motivations' as self-interest and ambition, and the more we are obliged to show, in terms of detailed and extended case histories, the working out of the courses of action that are set in train by these and like impulsion.' Marc Swartz (1966)

'The chief's court does not belong to the chief, it belongs to the people'[32]

A major challenge faced by Chief Tshivhase was to address the rivalry between civic movements and traditional rulers. In the preceding chapter I traced the origin and spread of civic associations in rural areas of South Africa and Tshivhase in particular. I have also referred to them several times in this chapter but now turn my focus to them with reference to specific cases.

As soon as I had immersed myself in the Tshivhase area, I discovered that the relationship between civic associations and traditional authorities had not always been amicable. Towards the end of the homeland period, the distinction between officeholders and the office of chief had become deeply blurred on account of the extreme unpopularity of many chiefs who owed their positions to the apartheid system. Civic associations had projected themselves as a democratic alternative to the institution of chief. On the one hand, traditional leaders and the elders were accused of having betrayed their people (especially the younger generation) by drifting along with the apartheid system. On the other hand, the chiefs and elders perceived civic members who were mostly youths as a company of unruly individuals who had no respect for 'tradition', and the elders of the chiefdom. The elders also accused the youths of having soiled their hands with blood by killing innocent men and women during the witchcraft uprisings of the late 1980s and early 1990s (see Ralushai Commission, 1996 for details on witchcraft murders and accusations in the Limpopo Province).

Most civic associations gained popularity in the Tshivhase chiefdom in 1990, which coincided with the military coup that brought Gabriel Ramushwana to power. Civic members tended to target headmen who had openly identified with the Venda National Party (VNP) or collaborated with the apartheid system in other ways. Although civic associations failed to overthrow the chiefs or to replace the system of chieftaincy, they continued to wield enormous influence in chiefdom affairs. In many cases, they claimed to be the 'true' representatives of the people and therefore allocated land and set up peoples' courts. According to them, the chiefs could continue with issues that concerned tradition and custom as long as the chiefs did not interfere with their activities.

But by 2001, it was evident that a lot of things had changed since 1994. In particular, the civics had diluted their hostility towards chiefs as a result of several factors, some of which have already been discussed above. However, there were a couple of stories of conflicts between chiefs and civic members in some villages prior to my arrival in Venda. The change in orientation among civics can be attributed to several factors, one being the way in which Chief Tshivhase has dealt with civic-chief relations in his chiefdom.

The first factor is that the membership of civic associations has changed since the early 1990s. I refer here to the fact that the actors today are not necessarily the same people who dominated the events of the late '80s and early 1990s.[33] Contemporary civic members do not share the memories of the actors in the 1980s. Except for a few who are much older now (in their early 40s), most of the civic members I encountered were young males either in their late teens or early 20s. Clearly, these new breed of civic members were preoccupied with a set of new challenges remotely related to those in the 1990s.

The second factor is Chief Kennedy Tshivhase's reconciliatory approach. Contrary to expectations that he would replace the headmen who had opposed his claim to the Tshivhase throne, or who were apartheid-era appointees, he chose instead to maintain them in office thereby stressing reconciliation and the unity of the chiefdom. His tough approach also extended to the incorporation of all voices (stakeholders) in decision-making circles such as the village councils. Although this was popular, some headmen were reluctant to put this in practice. This explains some of the isolated events that took place between 1998 and 2001 described below.

It also needs to be emphasised that Chief Tshivhase made strenuous efforts to placate the civics to his side. It was generally acknowledged in civic circles that Chief Tshivhase was a 'comrade' who understood the concerns of civic organisations. Some of the civic members hinted that they had been students with Kennedy Tshivhase at the University of the North in the 1980s and it was therefore expected of him to understand their position. But it is also significant that Kennedy Tshivhase initially identified himself with the ANC, and consequently with the objectives of the liberation movements. He also emphasised that in the early 1990s, he was a youth and therefore 'spoke the language of the youth'. As a prominent ANC member in Venda, Chief Tshivhase attempted to harmonise the South African Constitution with traditional leadership. One innovation was to make use of the TTC to undertake a campaign in the villages aimed at stimulating discussion and debate on the relationship between chiefs and civic organisations and their respective roles. In August 2001 Chief Tshivhase delivered a lecture at the University of Venda on chief - civic relations in which he emphasised the need for co-operation and accountability. According to a key informant, the campaign team emphasised that the civics were, first and foremost, the subjects of the chiefs:

Civics are the subjects of the chiefs. They are responsible for service delivery. Even formerly, this was the case, because the chief could not rule the country alone. In 1996, we were called to address the civics of a village in our chiefdom. They wanted to know about civics - chiefs relations. We insisted that we are working together and we would like you guys to tell us how this should be done. Most of the rebellious people were teachers who thought they were the one-eyed in the country of the blind. We also told them that what used to be the parliament of our forefathers, was the chief's court and if ever they had anything to discuss, they should go back to the chief's court. The chief's court does not belong to the chief, it belongs to the people. (Member of the campaign team of the Territorial Council, May 27 2001).

The TTC recognised the democratic input of the civics and suggested that their role was, among other things, to facilitate service delivery; that is, to act as intermediaries between chiefs and the grassroots. In order for them to play this role properly, the TTC argued, civics had to work closely with the village councils. Delivery, they maintained, could take place only if there was harmony between chiefs and civic structures. The chief's kraal was portrayed as the 'peoples' parliament', not the school or other venues where civic movements usually met. The Territorial Council also emphasised that the *chief's court did not belong to the chief, but to the people as a whole.* It was the meeting point of the forefathers, those who were living, and those yet to be born.

Lastly, developments in the late 1990s indicate that some of the policies of the local government in Thohoyandou have been unpopular not only with the chiefs, but also with civic members in both urban and rural areas. Many civic members feel sidelined by the new elite as demonstrated in the march against the municipal council in August 2001. Chief Tshivhase and his colleagues have therefore benefited from the low esteem that subjects have for the municipal council, given that the masses expect little from chiefs in terms of service delivery or job creation. The above factors contributed individually and collectively to a new 'alliance' between a majority of traditional leaders and civic movements in Tshivhase.

In April 2001 just a month before I commenced my research, members of the civics of Mukula requested Chief Tshivhase to intervene in an on-going conflict between them and the chief of their village. This was not the first conflict between them, but this particular case was threatening to escalate into severe violence. The headman resented the fact that the civic in his village undermined his authority. He had created a rival civic association, consisting of members loyal to him, because the members of the 'legitimate' civic did not want to stop allocating land or operating a people's court. On the other hand, the civic members argued that the headman had continuously kept them sidelined from his council and would not listen to their ideas. The headman's action proved counter-productive, given that soon after he had successfully established a civic group of loyal members, those who regarded themselves as the legitimate civic group began issuing death threats against him. Knowing that Chief Tshivhase was in favour of civic movements, the leaders of the civic association in Mukula requested him to remove the headman who was accused of being an obstacle to development. Chief Tshivhase called for a meeting of the disputing parties at the school where the independent civic usually met. Eventually, he succeeded in brokering a peace deal between the two groups. The headman was requested to dissolve his civic and restructure his village council to accommodate the independent civic. The latter also pledged, in turn, to collaborate with the headman and stop allocating land or solving disputes at the village school.

The second case took place in the village of Tshilidzini. In 1998 the headman of Tshilidzini decided to allocate a piece of land to a group of business persons who had plans to set up a business in the area. When the members of the local civic learnt of the headman's decision, they protested on the grounds that they were discussing an alternative plan for the land. They demanded that the headman should revoke his decision, but he stood his ground. When it became obvious that he would not concede to the demands of the civic members, the latter threatened to burn his kraal. They reminded the headman that as civics, they were the *true* representatives of the people in the village, not him. Who, they questioned, was the headman to decide on their behalf? The headman responded that he owned the land and could do with it as he wished. In discontent, some civic members threatened legal action against him while others terrorised him with death threats. Seeing the dangers ahead, the headman requested the mediation of Chief Tshivhase. Chief Tshivhase came to the assistance of the headman and after considering both sides of the matter, recommended that the headman should listen to his people and endeavour to work closely with them in order for development to prevail. The civic members, informants added, insisted on an apology from their headman, who reluctantly consented. The headman has since learnt to work closely with members of the civic in his village.

Members of the civic in Mukumbani have also had difficult times with their headman. The civic in Mukumbani was the most popular in the entire chiefdom. In the past couple of years, they have carried out a number of development projects that created employment opportunities for a small number of youths in the village. They have also had several conflicts with their headman, who came to power during the reign of the Regent. Informants recalled that the last minor conflict was in 1997 when the civic applied to Eskom (an electricity company) to electrify several houses in the village. As soon as the installations began, the headman intervened and asked the company to halt its activities in his village. He criticised the civic for not having discussed the issue with him before inviting Eskom. The headman promised civic members that he would pay a visit to Eskom and invite the company to install power in the specified stands but failed to keep to his promise. The headman also ran into trouble with civic members when he reported to Eskom that some people in his village had acquired and were using electricity illegally. Although the civic has had other minor conflicts with the headman, civic members attribute the absence of major trouble to Chief Tshivhase's diplomatic interventions.

As I pointed out earlier, the above incidents were isolated rather than characteristic of a general trend. In most villages, civic associations collaborated with their headmen and although they did not have the resources to serve as an alternative site of power, their contributions to tribal government were recognised. In Tshilungulu for instance, the civic met every Sunday at the local school but reported back to the headman. I attended several of their meetings and observed their deliberations. Most of them spoke very well of their headman while disparaging the local council authorities. Civic members were particularly proud of their headman for his material and financial contribution towards development initiative in the village. For example, informants pointed out that the headman had personally bought the pipes that were needed for the installation of pipe-borne water in the village. On the contrary, a civic member expressed his disillusionment with the local government:

> We are very much disappointed because if you come to our area and ask any person they will tell you they didn't know why they voted because we don't have anything. The council hasn't constructed the road to our place, they haven't delivered, in short, they've done nothing to show their presence in our area. (Civic member, Tshilungulu 15 July 2001).

The civic in Tshilungulu performed several functions. One of these was to co-ordinate discussions and visits to relevant government departments or service providers such as Eskom. In a particular example, the civic members were responsible for drawing up a list of those who wanted electricity, after which the list and the application letter were taken to the chief who stamped the documents before they were taken to Eskom. The civics also had a Tshivhase Development Forum (a small discussion group), whose primary purpose was to lobby funds for development projects in their village. The Forum worked closely with the headman and kept a record of their activities and applications.

Chief Tshihvhase and Public Opinion

I have argued in this chapter that some of the changes in Tshivhase are partly as a result of transformations in local government and partly due to Chief Tshivhase's personal dynamism. Chief Tshivhase has successfully extended his legitimacy to the headmen under him, in most cases by persuading them to toe the line. His legitimacy at the local level is consequently reinforced by his high profile status in the ANC at both national and provincial levels. Be that as it may, it is important to establish the extent to which the people have been persuaded by his claims to legitimacy and the nature of their reaction to his leadership. Thus, it is worth exploring the opinions that subjects held about Chief Tshivhase and what this meant in terms of the relationship between the chief and his subjects. Two broad categories of opinions on Chief Tshivhase are evident - partly on his political status and partly on his involvement in socio-cultural matters.

Political opinions about him dealt with his involvement in the politics of the democratic era on the side of the ANC. Although a young man, it is evident by now that Tshivhase is not new to the political landscape in South Africa and the Limpopo Province in particular. During one of my interviews with him, Tshivhase told me that Nelson Mandela had told him how much he was reminded of his grandfather, Ratsimphi, every time he saw him. This claim was in connection to the fact that Chief

Tshivhase's grandfather had been a communist activist in the 1940s and had personally known Mandela at the outset of the liberation struggle. I have already suggested in the preceding chapter that Tshivhase drew some kind of moral capital from the legacy of his popular grandfather. It is in this connection that the Tshivhases were often associated with 'liberation heroes' in contrast to the Mphephu dynasty.[34]

This notwithstanding, Chief Tshivhase has become an influential politician in both regional and national politics. As an influential member of the ANC in the Limpopo Province, his subjects spoke about him with profound respect. Subjects suggested that it was partly because of Chief Tshivhase's relative power and influence that he could stand up against the market-driven policies of the local government. Others pointed out that the local government had succeeded in getting away with its unpopular policies in other Venda chiefdoms but could not do the same in Tshivhase. This implied that had Chief Tshivhase not been a powerful politician, they would be suffering the same consequences as those in other chiefdoms. Consequently, many subjects spoke of the chief in very positive terms, not only for having made the right choices on their behalf, but also, for belonging to the 'right' camp. This was in connection to the popularity of the ANC in the Limpopo Province as a whole. Chief Tshivhase's regional popularity was recognised when Nelson Mandela visited his kraal at Mukumbani in 1997 but failed to do the same to the other chiefs such as the Mphephu or the Mphaphuli. Chief Tshivhase has therefore emerged prominent in chiefdom politics and is determined to maintain his dominance for as long as he can.

Subjects also reacted positively to his preoccupation with socio-cultural activities and the changes he has introduced in this area. In this respect I refer to his role in the promotion of traditional dances, his participation in modern forms of recreation such as football, and his attitude in general towards women and the youth. One of the main traditional dances which Chief Tshivhase claims to have revived is the *tshikona*- a very popular male dance that involves the use of flutes and a huge drum. *Tshikona* is performed during festivities and funerals. The dancers form a circle and dance in a uniform manner while orbiting around the circle. Many informants acknowledged that during the end of the Regent's reign, *tshikona* was rarely performed and many youths boycotted it owing to the Regent's unpopularity. But Chief Tshivhase claims that as soon as he assumed effective office, he realised that the Tshivhase people were in danger of losing their 'culture', so he sought to revive the dance. *Tshikona* was taught to young men who enrolled on a voluntary basis. He also introduced annual inter-village competitions in the chiefdom. In order to popularise *tshikona* among the youth, he organised a series of tours to Cape Town, Johannesburg and Durban with the Mukumbani Tshikona group during which they showcased their talents. Many parents and youths described Chief Tshivhase as a 'champion of tradition' in reference to his involvement in cultural revival. In 2001 he hosted a major Domba school[35] at his kraal in Mukumbani which was well attended and appreciated by the subjects. Parents were pleased with the fact that HIV/AIDS related issues were incorporated into the initiation school's curriculum. Thus the initiates graduated from the school having learnt not only how to fulfil their roles as 'proper Venda women', but also how to look after themselves in these 'dangerous times' as described by the parent of an initiate. The event was also covered in some regional and national press.[36]

Figure 3: Young boys performing the Tshikona dance in Venda

Youths also spoke well of Chief Tshivhase owing to his involvement in the management and promotion of the Black Leopards of Thohoyandou, a premier soccer league football club. The 'Black Leopards' is the only football team from Venda to have successfully made it to the elite soccer level in South Africa. The chief's association with this success has made him very popular not only among supporters of the club but also among young people in general.

Figure 4: Chief Tshivhase, centre, with staff leads a group of his headmen in dancing the Tshikona.

His popularity among civics and youths in general can also be illustrated by the role he played in taking sides with the civics during a conflict that erupted between them and the police. In April 2002, the police opened fire on hundreds of protesting youths in the Tshivhase village of Ngwenani ya Mapholi. Three of the youths died, including the leader of the civic association in the village. According to local accounts, the civic members of Ngwenani were protesting police leniency over an alleged suspect who was accused of having murdered a woman (for ritual purposes) from their village. Youths were outraged by the fact that for over a year after the murder took place and the case had been reported to the police, the suspect had not yet been apprehended. The conflict erupted again after a couple of young men discovered a human skull in a pond while fishing. The skull was taken to the Thohoyandou police station, which concluded after a series of forensic tests that the skull was a male's, contrary to popular anticipation that the skull belonged to the woman who had been brutally murdered a year earlier. According to local accounts, the people were convinced that the police was covering up for the suspect. The civic organisation therefore mounted a series of protest demonstrations in their village and at the police station. Chief Tshivhase is reported to have joined the protesting civics in the village and when the police threatened to open fire, informants claimed that he had asked to be shot in place of the young men. Chief Tshivhase and many of the civic members I talked to, claim that the people have lost confidence in the police. It is also popularly known that Chief Tshivhase tends to side with the civic, youths and women. Many women for instance applauded his decision to stop discrimination against them in matters of communal land allocation. Expectedly some men did not approve of this although critics have not challenged him overtly on this matter.

Chieftaincy and Development in Tshivhase

According to Bank and Southall (1996), traditional leadership has the potential of complementing or providing a powerful foundation upon which postcolonial African states can construct new experimental governments, including constitutional democracies. This study reveals that the institution of chief has the virtue of being close to marginalized groups and rural communities. As a matter of fact, chieftaincy is intricately embedded in the social structures of these groups. It does not follow that chiefs necessarily act in the interests of these communities or peoples. This study suggests that in Tshivhase, the chief has gained credibility among the people by positioning himself and acting in particular ways on behalf of the rural poor. He has accomplished this by exploiting the low esteem that the masses have for the local council by asserting his capacity to act decisively as both chief and ANC politician. Although he has done little to ameliorate the living conditions of his subjects, he has opposed local government policies that would have rendered their lives even worse. Evidence of this has been detailed above and can be contrasted with those in other Venda chiefdoms such as the Mphaphuli area.

The point is that the introduction of democracy in a neo-liberal age has led to new forms of exclusion particularly among the poor and rural populations, given the history of dispossession in South Africa and the present economic conditions. The popular assumption among the people was that the introduction of democratic local

[51]

government would open up space to previously excluded groups to gain access to similar kinds of services as those in urban areas. But what most of the rural population did not know or anticipate was that they would have to pay for these services the same as people in urban areas. When it eventually dawned on the rural poor that service consumption was beyond their reach, they began to oppose the market-orientated policy of the municipal authorities. This experience is not unique to Tshivhase. Similar trends have been observed in some rural and urban areas of South Africa (cf. Comaroff and Comaroff 2000:299).

I consider the above finding worthy of further analysis in the light of arguments which predicted doom for chiefs and chieftaincy in the post-apartheid context. Maloka (1996) for instance argued that although chiefs were determined to find a space for themselves in the new democratic dispensation, it was doubtful if they could extend 'popular participation' to the local level. He anticipated that recently elected local governments were more likely to play this role (Maloka 1996:193). But as seen in the details above, many years after the introduction of democratic local government, the plight of the masses are yet to be addressed. The municipal councils do not offer protection to the poor against the inequalities of the market but instead promote the discourse of neo-liberalism, which is not in the interest of the poor. For a parallel example, I will make reference to Nkuna's (2002) study in the Greater Tzaneen municipality already reviewed in chapter one. In summary, his study describes and analyses the conflict between the Greater Tzaneen municipal council and the rural population under chiefs. He contends that the municipality's market-driven policies provoked resentment among the rural poor partly because the municipal council failed to consult with the target population before implementing its policies. People were also angered by the exorbitant bills charged by the council. In many cases, the council charged an amount that was less than the citizens had consumed.

One can see from this example and the experience in Tshivhase that democracy is yet to become a way of life even among elected local government authorities. The above cases also show the continued relevance of chiefs in the democratic era despite attempts by local government officials to sideline them from post-apartheid politics. But the case of Chief Tshivhase illustrates the argument that not all chiefs have been successful in rehabilitating themselves in the new dispensation or have exploited the weaknesses of the local government to act decisively on behalf of the rural poor. Nkuna's (2002) chief for example is shown to have succeeded at least to some extent in gaining credibility with the masses for two reasons: one, because he cleared his name of the accusations that he had collaborated with the local council against the people and two, by requesting the people not to cooperate or pay any charges to the local council. This example and that of Chief Tshivhase in particular reveal the chief's capacity to demarcate a political space within which he can maintain control over his subjects and resources. Clearly, this is indicative of the contested postcolonial terrain as articulated by Maloka (1996).

The above issues notwithstanding, ethnographic data from Tshivhase suggest that there is an unresolved tension between the people's expectations of the new democratic dispensation and the lived reality on the ground. Comaroff and Comaroff (1999b) have grappled with these issues in their comments on the contradiction of democracy in the age of neo-liberalism. According to them, 'the end of apartheid held out the prospect that *everyone* would be set free to speculate and accumulate, to consume, and to indulge repressed desires. But for many, the millenial moment passed without palpable payback' (Comaroff and Comaroff 1999:284). This observation is true of Tshivhase as it is of other rural communities in South Africa. In fact, Richard Sandbrook had warned in the 1980s against what he termed the 'overly sanguine' anticipation that 'democratization will resolve problems of inequality and poverty' given that although in principle, electoral politics empowers the poor to demand reform in the distribution of income and wealth, in practice, the entrenched power of the oligarchy or dominant classes obstructs social and economic reform (Sandbrook 1988:143). Although the last contention is not necessarily true of Tshivhase, many scholars are of the opinion that democracy will make meaning to ordinary Africans depending on how 'it relates to the social experiences of Africans and how far it serves their social needs' (Ake 2000:75).

Others remain apprehensive about the co-existence of liberal democracy and economic neo-liberalism. Samir Amin for example observed that 'democracy...is incompatible with the demands of capitalist expansion' given that 'peripheral development could take no other course' thus aggravating rather than reducing social inequalities (Amin 1994:321-325). Recent studies on 'democratic' local government in South Africa seem to suggest that some local council authorities are not as democratic as they purport to be. Ntsebeza (1998) for example contends that the 'fact that they [municipal authorities] came to office through a process of democratic elections does not mean that they are necessarily honest. Recent reports suggest high levels of corruption, embezzlement of funds, nepotism and favouritism reminiscent of the corruption during the Bantustan era' (Ntsebeza 1998:161). Given the above, it is obvious that 'without adequate resources, responsibilities and legal capabilities' local government could easily become a 'mere talking shop' (Oluwu 1999:288).

Unless fundamental issues such as job creation and access to reserves and funds are addressed, the bulk of the rural population will be unable to exercise their economic citizenship. As a matter of fact, this observation is not limited to rural areas only, given the recent wave of protests in urban areas against privatisation and government's reluctance to address the problem of job losses.[37] In Tshivhase, many young people are still suffering from the effects produced by job losses following the closure of the few industries that were located in Shayandima in the early 1990s. No doubt, there has been much hostility towards local government's efforts to provide services to rural populations at a market price.

Conclusion

Two main conclusions can be drawn from this chapter. The first is that the socio-political changes that have occurred in Tshivhase since 1994 have also led to the 'transformation of the structures and relationships of power' (Goheen 1992:406). This is evident in Tshivhase's dealing with civic associations and the headmen under him. Old hostilities and relations of oppression have been deconstructed and in their wake, new relationships have been forged whereby groups and individuals previously sidelined from the affairs of the chiefdom have gained accommodation. By invoking the 'parliamentary' nature of the chief's *khoro* for example, Chief Tshivhase seems to

[53]

have harmonised the ideals of the new democratic dispensation with the realities in his chiefdom. In this connection, the chief's court has ceased being the *decentralised despot's forum* and has become a public forum where all and sundry can express their views. In the village of Tshilidzini, for example, as much as civics accepted their status as subjects, they demanded that their views should not be ignored in matters of land, and other public affairs. Chief Tshivhase's emphasis on including the civics as opposed to the local council's policy of excluding them has boosted his popularity and prominence in chiefdom politics. This can be attested to by the fact that many civic organisations invoked his mediation between them and their headmen. This is an indication that Tshivhase has not only claimed legitimacy but has also persuaded a large following about such claims.

The second issue deals with the idea that chiefs should be seen as protectors of the rural poor. Some scholars have suggested that chieftainship in contemporary South Africa has the potential or actual capacity to function as an institution of civil society, 'if not directly as an institution of government' (Thornton 2002:1). This particular argument is based on Thornton's research in the Barberton district of South Africa and has been raised in the Centre for Civil Society online discussion of the University of Natal. Although his work is unpublished, Thornton's argument implies that chiefs should be seen as protectors of the rural poor in the current democratic dispensation. This is based on his survey, which reveals that there is renewed and extensive support for the institution of chief in Barberton.

Thornton is not alone in this line of thought. Although not referring to South Africa in particular, Trutz von Trotha (1996) also argued that given the democratic transition in Africa, chieftaincy has become an 'institution of local justice, of public debate, and of an emerging civil society based on the traditions of African polities and institutions' (1996:92). It seems to me that these discussions have made the fallacy of considering all chiefs as the same and of implying that chieftaincy has the same meaning for subjects in different places. This study shows that legitimacy for chiefs today is a function of several factors, which must be clearly isolated for deep analysis. This legitimacy is to a large extent, a result of the contradictions of democracy in a neo-liberal age. But not all chiefs can claim this legitimacy because some have been irreparably tainted by past association with apartheid. Even in situations where the chiefs are newcomers, there is evidence that not all of them have been successful to the same extent. This could be seen in the case of the chief of Dan village in the Greater Tzaneen municipality (cf. Nkuna 2002). In the light of these findings, it is premature to argue that chiefs in general should be seen as protectors of the rural masses in the current democratic dispensation.

In the next two chapters, I will examine the case of fon Ganyonga of Bali in Cameroon with the intention of undertaking comparative analysis in chapter six. Although Ganyonga's career looks quite similar to that of Tshivhase, the reality is that Ganyonga became unpopular in the democratic era for gaining prominence by virtue of his involvement in the politics of the ruling party. Although he initially lost considerable legitimacy in the eyes of his own people, he subsequently won some credibility with them by participating with other chiefs to call for a solution to the 'Anglophone problem'. Ganyonga's case is therefore not only a contradictory one, but also complex. However, the question to keep in mind (and which will be examined more profoundly in chapter 6) is whether Cameroon is following the predictions about the incompatibility of chiefs and democracy, whereas South Africa is not.

Chapter Four

Historical patterns on change and continuity in traditional leadership in Bali

Introduction

This chapter examines in brief, the migration history of the Chamba group during the 18th century and its present circumstances, particularly since the early 1990s. It examines the disintegration of the Chamba group into several chiefdoms, one of them being Bali Nyonga and its implications for understanding inter-chiefdom politics in the present North West Province of Cameroon. Unlike the chiefdoms of Venda, no dominant authority sought to reunite the Chamba under a single leader thereafter, although Bali Nyonga chiefs emerged more powerful than their counterparts during the colonial episode partly because of their relative military strength as well as their alliance with German colonialists.

Bali Nyonga's history is examined alongside the history of the state in Cameroon. It demonstrates that the consolidation of the postcolonial state under the authoritarian regime of Ahmadou Ahidjo was somehow accompanied by policies aimed at sidelining chiefs in local and national politics. This period also saw the emergence of new bureaucratic elite that sought to dominate local and regional affairs. With the demand for democratic reform gathering momentum in the 1980s and the eventual commencement of political liberalisation in 1990, traditional leaders began to reclaim the space they had lost over the decades.

A primary objective of this chapter is to provide the reader with a sketch of the history of Bali chiefs and how their political actions became entangled with that of the colonial and postcolonial states. I also seek to show how and why fon Ganyonga became involved in national politics, particularly within the structures of the ruling party, the CPDM. This chapter sets a stage for the reader's understanding of the kinds of legitimacy that Ganyonga claims in the democratic era (discussed in detail in chapter five). I also emphasise that although the contexts have changed, there is continuity in the ways that successive Bali chiefs have claimed legitimacy by aligning themselves with dominant centres of power. Even though this has undermined their popularity in the eyes of the people at one stage or another, they have, nonetheless, succeeded in maintaining dominance in regional politics.

A Political History of Bali Nyonga

Bali Nyonga, commonly known as Bali, belongs to the Chamba group that migrated from the Chamba area of what is today known as Northern Cameroon to the Bamenda grasslands.[38] The date of their exodus is not certain but could be estimated to the beginning of the second quarter of the 19th century (Hunt 1925). Historical accounts hold that the Chamba were the last of the ethnic groups to settle in the grasslands of Bamenda in the second half of the 19th century (Nyamndi 1988; Chilver and Kaberry 1967; Kaberry and Chilver 1961).

Under the leadership of Gawolbe, the Chamba group arrived at Banyo in about 1825 where they incorporated other groups such as the Peli, Mboum, Buti and Tikar. The Chamba and its new allies continued their journey further south and settled near the powerful Bamum kingdom, which today is found in the Western Province. There, the Chamba tried to subjugate the Bamum with the aid of the Bati, a small group that had been suffering constant persecution from the Bamum. Although the Chamba failed to defeat the Bamum, they incorporated some of the Bati and continued their march southwards. They crossed the river Nun and entered the Bamenda grasslands where they fought with the already established kingdoms of Mankon, Bafut, Pinyin, Meta and Moghamo. Unable to find a territory to settle (without opposition from the neighbouring groups), the Chamba left the Bamenda grasslands and moved further west into Dschang, located in the present-day Western Province. There, their leader, Gawolbe was killed in battle forcing the group to retreat southwards to Bagam where they reorganised and selected a new leader (Nyamndi 1988:29-32).

Gangsin succeeded Gawolbe in about 1836 but his unpopularity and inability to sustain the cohesion of the large group triggered a struggle for the throne. Owing to the fact that none of Gawolbe's sons was able to emerge as the dominant successor, the group eventually split into seven separate factions led by each of the six sons and one daughter. The seven groups were Bali-Kumbat which eventually settled in the Ndop plains in the Bamenda grasslands, Bali-Gangsin presently found south-east of Bali-Kumbat, Bali-Gashu also located east of Bali-Kumbat, Bali-Gham located near Santa, Bali-Muti found in the Tabara State of Nigeria, Bali-Kontan which was later incorporated by Bali-Nyonga and finally, Bali-Nyonga located near Mankon. Except Bali-Muti, all the other factions migrated back to the Bamenda grasslands where they settled permanently.

'Of these sections Bali Nyonga had the largest following with Bali-Kumbat as his most formidable rival' (Hunt 1925:9). Gawolbe's only daughter, Nanyonga led the Bali Nyonga group taking with her most of the Bati, Tikali, Buti, Peli and Kufat that had been incorporated over the years. This accounts for the composite nature of Bali Nyonga, which includes non-Chamba elements from within and beyond the grasslands (Fowler and Zeitlyn 1996). Nanyonga later handed over power to her son Nyongpasi who became the first fon of Bali and was known as Fonyonga I.[39]

About 1855, Fonyonga moved to Kufom, a site not far from the present Bali Airport, at that time occupied by Bali-Kontan that had arrived at the area much earlier. Bali-Kontan was subjugated and incorporated into the Bali Nyonga group and its leader compensated with the office of sub-chief under Fonyonga I. Other neighbouring groups such as the Baku and the Kenyang were also incorporated into Bali Nyonga. A year later, Fonyonga I died and his son Galega I succeeded him as the new fon of Bali-Nyonga. Galega I later moved his palace to the present capital in about 1875 where he devoted his time in expanding and constructing a strong centralised state (Titanji et al. 1988).

Whilst Galega I was busy consolidating his authority in Bali, several developments were going on at the coast, about 300 miles away. In July 1884 the coastal chief of the Douala, Chief Manga Bell signed a treaty with the German representative, General Nachtigal (Chem-Langhëë 2004; Chiabi 1997). This treaty made Douala and the surrounding hinterlands a German protectorate. However the Germans unilaterally decided to expand their territorial claims beyond the areas stipulated in the treaty – an expansion that was spearheaded by one of their explorers. On 16 January 1889 Dr Eugen Zintgraff, a German explorer arrived at Bali where he stayed for four months and built a German station (O'neil 1996). He signed a blood pact of friendship with Galega I and also took a Bali woman as wife. It should be noted that by the time of Zintgraff's arrival, Galega was not on friendly terms with some of the powerful chiefs of the grasslands due to his expansionist ambitions and also because the Chamba had attacked them before during their search for a site to settle.

When Zintgraff visited Bafut later in 1889 and belittled the Bafut fon,[40] Galega was blamed for instigating Zintgraff to behave in this manner. Relations between the Germans and the Bafut fon deteriorated and eventually resulted in armed conflict. Although Galega helped the Germans in their attempt to subjugate the Bafut, it is evident that such assistance was related to Galega's territorial ambitions in the grassfields. In August 1891 Zintgraff reached an agreement with Galega which recognised and safeguarded the interests of each party, even though critics have pointed out Zintgraff's intentions to dupe the Bali fon (cf. Nyamndi 1988:132). The agreement read as follows:

The exercise of all power over the Bali lands is transferred by Garega (sic) to Dr. Zintgraff so far as Garega disposes of such power at the time being, namely, the power of life and death over the Bali people as also the exclusive decision over peace and war. In return for the above *Garega is assured of the establishment, recognition and protection of his position as paramount chief over the surrounding tribes of the northern hinterland of the Cameroons.*[41] (My emphasis)

For a long time, Galega became the dominant political figure in the grasslands through his alliance with the Germans to further his own interests. Consequently, Bali became the centre of trade in the grasslands as German traders frequently made trips to Bali to sell their goods and buy local products such as ivory and carved products. In 1901 Fonyonga II requested the Germans to build a Basel mission station. This was accomplished in 1903 and two pioneer missionaries were sent to cater for the interests of the mission. The church is still surviving today and continues to attract Protestant worshippers throughout the grasslands. The first modern school was also built soon after the church had been completed. This consolidated Bali as the centre of German activity in the grasslands (Bali-Nyonga History and Culture Committee 1986:9). Furthermore, the German missionaries adopted Mungaka, the Bali Nyonga language as the principal medium of evangelisation.[42] Mungaka was subsequently introduced in formal schooling and soon became a lingua franca in the entire grasslands. By 1915 the Basel missionaries had already translated sections of the Bible into Mungaka.

Meanwhile, Zintgraff died in December 1897 on his way back to Germany. Galega outlived him for a few years and died in 1901. He was succeeded by his son, Tita Gwenjang who was crowned Fonyonga II. Fonyonga was the one who requested the Basel Mission to set up a station in Bali. After the German imperialists had conquered the powerful chiefdoms of Mankon and Bafut, the new challenge was to administer the grasslands. Once again, they had to rely on the Bali chief for this purpose. In 1903 the German colonial Governor, Puttkamer acknowledged Fonyonga II's 'faithful services' and granted him 'full protection of the Imperial Government'. The Governor provided further that all colonial officials and other Europeans residing in Bali or travelling through it were expected to 'pay their respect to the defence given him and always to be willing to afford Chief Fonyonga of Bali every possible assistance' (Nyamndi, 1988:108).

On 15 June 1905 in the assembly of 47 grasslands fons, General Hauptmann Glauning (a German emissary) formally installed Fonyonga II at Bali as paramount chief of 31 non-Bali villages (Hunt, 1925:13). In turn the Germans expected two principal functions from Fonyonga: to collect taxes and to recruit labour for the plantations at the coast.[43] This new role later complicated relations between Fonyonga II and his subordinate chiefs. For instance in 1906 the Germans brutally resettled eleven Meta villages into Bali territory to ensure the smooth collection of taxes and in 1910 the chief of Batibo was exiled to Banyo for insubordination to Fonyonga (Nyamndi, 1988:110). These developments placed Fonyonga at the centre of controversy leading to his unpopularity among some non-Bali villages. Gradually the Germans fell out with Fonyonga and returned most of the vassal chiefdoms back to independence. This decline in their relations continued until the Germans were expelled during the First World War. The German military station that had been erected in Bamenda fell to the Allied Forces in 1915.

After Germany's defeat and expulsion, Britain and France jointly administered the territory for a short while although the two powers later divided the Protectorate into two separate territories. This division was confirmed with minor adjustments by the Milner-Simon agreement of July 1919(Chem-Langhëë 2004; Chiabi 1997). As a result, Bali fell into the British zone. Once the British took over Bamenda in January 1916,[44] Fonyonga II produced a list of several villages under his control and promptly sent a 'fine elephant tusk to His Majesty the King [of England], who sent in return an autographed portrait' (Hunt 1925:19). Although the fon's control over the other non-Bali villages continuously waned, the District Officer noted his intention and determination 'to restore as far as the principles of Native Administration permit the position of the Bali chief as the most influential chief of the countryside, so *that he may regain in moral prestige what he has lost in manpower*' (emphasis mine).

Most of the British administrators were pleased with Fonyonga II partly for his help in defeating the Germans but also because of his relative dominance in the grassfields. The first D.O. for instance described Bali as 'the most advanced of the various tribal divisions' in the Bamenda grasslands. His successor, N.C. Duncan, later described Fonyonga II as the 'most intelligent and farseeing native gentleman whom I have encountered during eighteen years spent in West and South Africa'.[45] Soon after the British had taken over, they instituted a new form of local government by creating Native Authorities. Bali Nyonga became an important Native Authority and was credited with the first Native Authority school in the Bamenda grasslands. This was soon followed by the establishment of a Native Court in 1925.

When Fonyonga II died in August 1940 he was succeeded by his son, Vincent Samdala who was crowned Galega II and is remembered principally for his leading role in the struggle for independence. Galega II became an eminent politician in the British Cameroons (also known as the Southern Cameroons) and attended many of the conferences that were held to discuss the future of the Southern Cameroons. Although he was initially on good terms with the Premier of the British Cameroons, Dr. E

Endeley, he soon fell out with him owing to Endeley's disrespect for traditional rulers. In the 1940s he joined the coastal chief, Manga Williams, to represent the Southern Cameroons in the Regional Legislature at Enugu, Nigeria.[46] This position placed Galega II as an influential politician in the nationalist movement for independence and re-unification with East (French) Cameroon. Some of the important conferences in which he participated were the Mamfe Conference of 1953 and the 1957 Nigerian Constitutional Conference at Lancaster House, London. It was at the latter conference that he expressed his support for re-unification with French Cameroon, thereby tilting the balance of power in favour of Dr John Ngu Foncha, who was then the leader of the opposition party in the British Cameroons. Upon his return to Bali, he campaigned quite forcefully for his people to vote for the Re-unification Movement led by Foncha. The other camp led by Endeley advocated independence by joining Nigeria.

Galega II was also credited for being the architect of the Southern Cameroon House of Chiefs. This is understandable since he introduced the idea from his experience in Nigeria. Upon its formation the Bafut fon headed the House while he became the vice-president. Southern Cameroons eventually got its independence through reunification with East Cameroon on 1 October 1961. Thereafter, a two-state Federal Republic was established headed by President Ahmadou Ahidjo.

Galega II in the Post-independence Era (1961-1985)

There is further need to explore Galega II's tenure as chief during the first half of the postcolonial era because it is intertwined with the history of postcolonial Cameroon and the general position of traditional rulers. It will become evident that although the postcolonial state sought to reduce chiefs' power, Galega II still made use of the changing political landscape to claim new legitimacy and foster his own political interests.

As stated earlier, the Federal Republic was composed of two states: West Cameroon (formerly Southern Cameroons) and East Cameroon (formerly *La Republique du Cameroun*). West Cameroon was economically less developed than the East but had a more pluralistic and participatory political system when contrasted with the centralised system of East Cameroon (Gabriel 1999). Initially, there was concerted effort to develop the economic potentials of West Cameroon through the construction of roads, schools, and hospitals (Eyongetah and Brain 1974), ironically, accompanied by the simultaneous dismantling of strategic energy, water and banking infrastructures (Konings and Nyamnjoh 2003; Mukong 1990; Atanga 1994). With regular French aid, Cameroon was able to register stable economic growth and prosperity. Ironically, it was the peace and stability enjoyed by Cameroon that provided the basis for authoritarian rule, not excluding the ideological factors such as the protection of national unity in a profoundly diverse country - especially along ethnic and linguistic lines[47] (Eyongetah and Brain 1974:142).

Cameroon's first president, Ahmadou Ahidjo provided the ideological rhetoric for a strong, centralised and unitary state by proposing the dissolution of political parties in West Cameroon to form a single party state. He achieved this in 1966 following the emergence of the *Union Nationale Camerounaise* (UNC) as the sole legal party in the Federal Republic. This was followed soon by the abolition of the federal structure in

May 1972, and replaced by a unitary state known as the United Republic of Cameroon. The collapse of the federal structure simultaneously saw the demise of several pluralistic structures in West Cameroon. One of the casualties of this period was the House of Chiefs, which entailed the relegation of chiefs to the background in national politics. Once the unitary state was put in place, Ahidjo made progress to consolidate authoritarian rule through effective centralisation of state power, assisted by a handful of politicians and new bureaucratic elite from the different regions of the country. This became effective to the extent that the distinction between the state and the party was more or less blurred. State institutions and the UNC were used to further the hegemonic project of dominant groups such as politicians, civil servants and business elite (Eyoh 1998b; 2004).

After abolishing the House of Chiefs in 1972, Ahidjo issued a presidential decree in 1977, which sought to define the role of chiefs in the 'nation-building' project. Critics have observed that the decree was controversial precisely because it sought to co-opt chiefs as clients into a largely patrimonial system (Jua 1995; Fisiy 1995). This decree remains the principal official document that defines the role of chiefs in Cameroon to date. Article 20 of Presidential Decree No. 77/245 of 15 July 1977 stipulated that recognised 'chiefs were to act as auxiliaries of the administration.' Their job, among other things, consisted of serving as 'intermediaries between the administration and the people, helping the administrative authorities in the execution of government directives and recovering state taxes within their domains' (Jua 1995:43). Article 2 of the decree went further to classify chiefdoms in terms of their relative power and influence. To this effect, three types of chiefdoms were outlined. First degree chiefs[48] were those with two Second Degree chiefs under their jurisdiction, which extended over a so-called divisional unit. Second Degree Chiefs were expected to have the allegiance of two Third Degree chiefs and their jurisdiction could be no larger than a sub-division. The jurisdiction of Third Degree Chiefs was limited to a village or a 'quarter' in a rural or urban area (Jua 1995:43). In accordance with colonial policy, they were also paid a monthly salary in addition to a small commission of tax collection, which has dwindled over the years after some of the basic taxes were abolished.

Prior to exercising their functions as auxiliaries of the administration, the decree recommended that an 'express note of administrative recognition' needed to be granted. Article 29 even carried threats of sanctions in case of non-compliance. Thus, it was not unusual to hear of fons being threatened or punished for not cooperating with the administration. For instance one can cite the Prefectoral order which forbade the fon of 'Nso' to leave his palace, as penalty for supporting his subjects in their refusal to pay water bills to a parastatal that had taken over their supply system (Jua 1995:43). In another example, the fon of Fungom was jailed arbitrarily in 1997 for supporting his people in their confrontation with Fulani graziers who had destroyed their farming fields.

Although the Chieftaincy Law of 1977 revealed 'the State's hegemonic project to co-opt traditional rulers into an already burdensome bureaucracy' (Fisiy 1995) it was evident that chiefs (especially grassfields chiefs) had lost their privileged role in national affairs. It was up to individual chiefs to look for new means of making their influence felt in local and regional politics.

[61]

In this regard, Galega II was quite shrewd. He quickly embraced the idea of a single national party and became a leading regional leader of the UNC. In fact, he was the first-section president for the UNC branch in the Mezam division. This administrative division (to which Bali still belongs) consists of two other powerful grassfields fons, namely the fons of Mankon and Bafut. Galega's influence as a politician was recognised in local and regional circles. This was evident when President Ahidjo paid an official visit to Galega at his palace in Bali. Galega II is also credited for having secured the elevation of Bali to a sub-division in Mezam division (Bali-Nyonga History and Culture Committee 1986:14).

Galega II passed away in September 1985 and for the first time in Bali history, a late fon's will was used to choose a successor. Galega had willed that his son Dohsang Galega should succeed him and this was executed with limited opposition. The new fon chose to call himself Ganyonga III (Nyamndi 1988:153). Although most subjects knew very little about him owing to his long stay abroad, it was anticipated that a highly educated chief of his calibre would successfully lead the chiefdom into the 21st century. The subjects also presented to him a brand new Mercedes car as tribute.

Ahidjo voluntarily resigned in 1982 and appointed Paul Biya, Prime Minister since 1975, as his successor. Although Ahidjo retained the position of chairman of the state party, he apparently developed nostalgia for power and sought unsuccessfully to amend the Constitution whereby the state would be subjected to or made an instrument of party-defined policy. In April 1984, a coup d'état, led by presidential guards mostly from Ahidjo's northern region, failed in what was popularly believed to be Ahidjo's desperate attempt to come back to office. The failed coup provided Paul Biya with enough excuses to purge his regime of Ahidjo's leftovers thus establishing a new configuration in Cameroon's political order. He also renamed the country from the United Republic of Cameroon to the *Republic of Cameroon* (the name borne by the former East Cameroon) (cf. Mbaku and Takougang 2004). In March 1985 Biya replaced the UNC with the Cameroon Peoples' Democratic Movement (CPDM). This was interpreted as Biya's final purge of Ahidjo's remnants and the consolidation of his New Deal government. Biya's consolidation and dominance of the new single party simultaneously saw the emergence of a bureaucratic elite from his ethnic group, the Beti, located in the Centre, South and Eastern provinces of Cameroon (Eyoh 1998b; 2004).

Biya's tenure in office was characterised by a reversal in economic prosperity and growth that had depended much on oil revenue (Jua 1993). Biya's poor performance can be contrasted to the annual growth of 6-7% GNP in the 1970s during Ahidjo's leadership (Rowlands and Warnier 1988:119). The decline of the economy reinforced resort to kinship and regional politics, provoking even fiercer competition for diminishing state resources. Corruption also worsened under Biya as the bureaucratic elite and politicians from his ethnic group publicly contended that it was their turn to monopolise the 'dining table.' With declining conditions of material subsistence, the legitimacy of the authoritarian state was greatly eroded and a growing sense of dissent began to dominate public discussion. This situation worsened between 1987 and 1990 provoking greater demand for the liberalisation of political space (Eyoh 1998b).

Although Biya was reluctant to heed the concerns of the population, John Fru Ndi braved the odds in May 1990 and launched the first major opposition party, the Social

Democratic Front (SDF) (Gwellem 1996). This triggered more demand for democratic reform compelling the state to liberalise political competition and the press in December 1990. Biya's reluctance to meet the increasing demand for democratic change further provoked over half a year of civil disobedience championed by leading opposition parties and civic movements. This period was popularly known as 'Ghost Towns' or *Villes Mortes*[49] in French. Eventually Biya consented to the pressure and opted to host the 'Tripartite Conference', a flawed mimicry of the Sovereign National Conference that was held in many Francophone countries in the early 1990s. Although the talks yielded little dividend, it paved the way for legislative and presidential elections in March and October 1992 respectively.

Fon Ganyonga and the Democratic Transition in 1990

1990 was a turning point not only for civil society and many political actors but also for traditional leaders. Soon after the SDF had been launched, Paul Biya backtracked on a promise he had made earlier in the year, specifically to exclude chiefs from active participation in party politics.[50] This became clear in July 1990 when he appointed Ganyonga and the fons of Mankon and Bafut into key positions of the CPDM. According to the appointments, Solomon Angwafor III of Mankon became the first Vice National President of the CPDM[51] and the fons of Bali and Bafut became alternate members of the Central Committee of the party. The Central Committee consisted of elite members of the party from all regions of the country and was second in importance to the Political Bureau.

The reintroduction of multiparty democracy offered enormous space for chiefs to play, once again, an important role in local and national politics. The appointment of Ganyonga and the other chiefs immediately raised their political status to the national level. This development also provided a major opportunity for Ganyonga in particular to play a prominent role in regional politics as his father had done in the 1950s during the struggle for independence and later in the 1970s as the divisional president of the UNC.

But the chiefs' new status in the CPDM and consequently, their overt participation in party politics triggered substantial debate on the role and status of traditional rulers in the new democratic dispensation. Initial reactions to the chiefs' appointment were generally bitter against Paul Biya and the CPDM government. Biya was accused of trying to destroy or undermine the powerful chiefs of the grassfields (for whom he allegedly had no respect) by politicising their role.[52] The newly independent and critical press frequently carried articles authored by members of civil society and subjects of the chiefs in which they condemned the fons for allowing themselves to be manipulated by the Biya government. 'By accepting to be dragged into partisan politics,' one newspaper argued 'it goes without saying that these fons have abdicated from their roles of impartial referees in the impending multiparty competition expected to begin soon in the country.'[53] Other critics of the decision assumed that Biya had made this move as a strategy to win future votes through the influence of the powerful and respected chiefs of the grasslands. A columnist wondered: 'hasn't it ever occurred to the CPDM leaders that these fons govern a traditionally democratic people whose thinking cannot be done for them by the fons?'[54] But *Cameroon Tribune*, the government controlled daily saw things from a less critical perspective. It applauded Biya's decision as worthy and decisive, completely in harmony with the spirit of the democratic transition: 'there is nothing more reasonable' it contended 'than giving credit where it is due. Our ancestral custodians should not fight battles to get what is naturally theirs.'[55] In other words, the co-optation of the chiefs into prominent positions in the ruling party was expected to reinforce their influence at the local level rather than undermine it. Consequently two diametrically opposed camps emerged. On the one hand, those who strongly advocated the neutrality (exclusion) of chiefs in party politics, and on the other, those who argued that chiefs should participate freely in party politics. A leading member of the latter camp was fon Angwafor III of Mankon. As the Vice President of the ruling CPDM he was very vocal about the democratic right of chiefs to be involved actively in any party of their choice:

> How can you deprive a citizen of involvement in politics simply because he holds a traditional title of *Fon*? The traditional ruler cannot be excluded from anything - politics, farming, trading, teaching, business and so forth. It is unthinkable to say chiefs should remain neutral in politics.[56]

This view was supported by many chiefs including Ganyonga. The Meta chief, fon Teche Mbah II, for instance argued that:

> I personally see nothing wrong in supporting a given political party. Since a *Fon* has the right to participate in politics, he equally has the right to support any party of his choice. Is there anything wrong if we decide to support the CPDM? If we support the CPDM, it is in order to attract development to our areas.[57]

These views have been contested since 1990 to date, but Ganyonga and his colleagues have maintained their position in the party and have succeeded in co-opting previously reluctant chiefs into the ruling party. His involvement in national politics and specifically on the side of the ruling party has brought his political legitimacy into question. It is thus important to ask what has brought about these changes? What kinds of legitimacy is the fon claiming, who is persuaded or not, and why? However, before we address these questions, it is necessary to explore some of the contentious political issues that became dominant during the democratic transition. These issues affected both subjects and traditional rulers.

Political liberalisation created space for the articulation of perceived or actual injustices by groups and communities that had been reluctant to do so during the authoritarian period. Foremost among these was the rise in Anglophone objection to what was popularly perceived as Francophone domination and the latter's attempts to re-colonise the Anglophone population. The history of the post-1990 era in Cameroon is replete with numerous Anglophone lobby groups advocating different and sometimes conflicting solutions to what has become known as the 'Anglophone problem'. This will be discussed in detail in the next chapter.

Another issue that became discernible was the ethnicisation of political parties. This was a situation whereby major political parties tended to have their greatest support in the home areas of the leaders or founders. Although Cameroon had over a hundred political parties by the end of 1992, only 4 major parties were existing. One was the ruling CPDM of Paul Biya which was perceived to be a *Beti*-dominated party (the President's ethnic group). The second was the SDF of John Fru Ndi, considered to be an Anglo-Bamileke grouping (dominated by people from the Northwest and Western provinces). The third was the Union Nationale pour la Démocratie et le Progrès (UNDP) of Belo Bouba Maïgari with a huge following among the Hausa-Fulani of Northern Cameroon, and finally the fourth, the Union Démocratique Camerounaise (UDC) of Ndam Njoya which enjoyed much support among the Bamum in the Sultanate of Foumban in the West Province (Eyoh 1998b)

The balkanisation of political competition became apparent during the presidential elections of October 1992 in which the incumbent, Paul Biya scored 39% of the vote, Fru Ndi of the SDF 35%, and Belo Bouba of the UNDP 19%. Biya drew his support mainly from the Centre, South, and Eastern Provinces while Fru Ndi commanded a following in the Northwest, Littoral, West and Southwest provinces. Finally, Belo Bouba captured the votes in the northern region of Adamawa although he had to compete for votes with Paul Biya in the other two Northern Provinces.

The post-1990 era has also been characterised by the decline in the nation-building project. In its wake, there has been an increased reversion to the politics of belonging and ethnic forms of identity and solidarity (Geschiere and Konings 1993; Nyamnjoh 1999; Bayart, Geschiere, and Nyamnjoh 2001; Eyoh 1998a, 2004). This constitutes an obsession with the exclusion of the *other* or the stranger from what is perceived to be an area or resource exclusive to the indigenous or autochthonous populations (Geschiere and Nyamnjoh 2000). Although this view is not widely apparent in the grasslands, the emergence of the discourse of autochthony has provided an enabling environment for the resurgence of chiefs in regional and national politics. By posing as the protectors or guarantors of the rights of their subjects, some chiefs have appropriated the discourse of democracy and autochthony to secure advantages for themselves and their regions.

Conclusion

This chapter, although historical in theme and purpose also sought to answer the following question: why has Ganyonga used his position as chief as a springboard into national politics? By means of secondary sources and analysis, I have shown that two main factors account for his involvement in national politics. First, that he was co-opted into the central committee of the ruling party thus bringing him into national prominence. Second, (although this is not yet fully evident at this stage), that it was in his own interests to join the ruling party, given the 'cosmetic' nature of the democratic transition in Cameroon and the atmosphere of political uncertainty in the country.

Nonetheless, the historical analysis reveals that chiefs in Bali have tended to align themselves with more powerful political forces to foster their own interests. This can be witnessed in Galega's pact with Zintgraff, Fonyonga's collaboration with the British, Galega II's prominence under Ahidjo and finally, Ganyonga's involvement in contemporary politics on the side of the CPDM. This shows that although the contexts have changed, there is clear continuity in the ways in which chiefs in Bali have coped with the challenges facing their status and institution. Ganyonga's involvement in national politics has provoked hostility towards the idea that chiefs should participate overtly in party politics. This hostility has been expressed in many ways, thereby questioning his claim to legitimacy in the domain of modern politics in the democratic era. In the next chapter, I will explore and analyse the nature of Ganyonga's claims to legitimacy and show how his relationship with his subjects has changed since 1990.

Chapter Five

Democratic transition and chiefdom politics in Bali

Introduction

The introduction of political pluralism in Cameroon in 1990 created conditions for the return of old political actors such as chiefs to the 'national political scene', despite the popular demand for 'actors' of a new kind (Geschiere 1993:151). The principal question was on what legitimacy would such 'old actors' play the politics of the democratic era? Would their claim be based on 'tradition' or on the grounds desired by the people for their new political actors? In many cases, traditional rulers attempted the two, claiming legitimacy on the basis of their status as 'natural rulers' and claiming to seek the welfare of their people. Fon Ganyonga was one of such chiefs whose political career gained prominence in 1990 following his co-optation into the ranks of the ruling CPDM. He was one of the 'old actors' clad in 'new clothes'. But the government's claim to legitimacy, owing to its introduction of political pluralism, was soon brought into question. It followed that similar claims made by 'old-new actors' such as Ganyonga also came into question. This was because the government and the CPDM party in particular were perceived as obstacles towards genuine democratic transformation in Cameroon. The people and the opposition expected traditional rulers to be 'neutral' mediators in the on-going struggle between civil society and the state, but this was not the case. Thus, many people expressed hostility not only towards their chiefs who sided with the state, but also to the idea of chiefs`s overt participation in multiparty politics.

This chapter examines the different claims to legitimacy by fon Ganyonga and how the people reacted to these claims. I argue that although Ganyonga's claim to legitimacy as a modern politician has been contested by many of his subjects, he has succeeded to win some measure of legitimacy because of his involvement in other political issues popular among the people. Nevertheless, his involvement in local and national politics has provoked different, and sometimes conflicting reactions from his subjects.

Democratic Transition and Local Politics in Bali

Ganyonga's involvement in local politics has been the subject of much controversy. His claim to legitimacy in the sphere of modern politics can be discerned in three broad areas: his abortive bid for the mayoral office in Bali in 1996, his prominence in chiefs' politics in the grasslands, and his lobby among chiefs in support of the 'Anglophone cause'. As indicated earlier, some of these claims have been rejected by the people while others have received approval and support. At issue here is the view that although Ganyonga failed to provide a shield for his people against the state, he succeeded to use his status as traditional ruler to articulate some of the concerns of the people.

Since 1990 Bali has been host to competing political interests and personalities. The on-going contest is between two principal parties, the ruling CPDM and the powerful opposition party, the SDF. I have already observed that the re-introduction of party politics in 1990 served as a strategic entry point for many chiefs who had played a relatively dormant role in local and/or national affairs before this era. Party politics and elections therefore offered a great opportunity for chiefs, not only to participate in the *invention* of Cameroon's future per se, but also, to safeguard and enhance their individual and collective interests. Based on my observations and archival data, this contention is as true of other regional chiefs as it is of fon Ganyonga.

Soon after its formation in 1990 the SDF became a very popular party not only in the North West Province, but also in the Western, Littoral and South West Provinces. Given the widespread popularity of the newly formed party, traditional leaders such as Ganyonga as well as the CPDM government, were perceived as obstructions to the wishes of the people. Although he continued to enjoy the support of some of the Bali elite and notables, the chances of the CPDM winning future elections in Bali were slim. The first multiparty parliamentary election was held in March 1992. This was boycotted by several opposition parties especially the SDF for want of an independent electoral commission. The SDF and its fellow opposition parties argued that without an independent body to organise and declare the results, the CPDM government would manipulate and outmanoeuvre the opposition by rigging – given that the CPDM was both player and umpire. The SDF's boycott led to a CPDM victory in all 20 parliamentary seats in the North West. Although most of the new parliamentarians were long-standing politicians, the fon of Bali-Kumbat made a fresh entry to parliament, thus opening the way for other fons to stand as candidates in future elections.

In October 1992 the much-awaited presidential election was held. Since 1990, no election in Cameroon has attracted as much fervour and enthusiasm as this one. Although the CPDM government insisted on organising the election (without an independent electoral commission) the SDF and other opposition parties decided not to squander another opportunity by boycotting as they had done in March 1992. Given the growing unpopularity of the CPDM, many people anticipated the inevitable demise of Paul Biya, but to everyone`s dismay he emerged victorious. Popular belief is that victory was stolen from Fru Ndi. The results showed that Paul Biya, the incumbent, won 39% of the votes, while Fru Ndi of the SDF and Belo Bouba of the UNDP won 35% and 19% respectively. Owing to violent protests in Bamenda and other parts of the North West, where the SDF commanded overwhelming support, a state of emergency was declared in the province which lasted over two months. Fru Ndi was also put under house arrest for declaring himself the president-elect.

This period was extremely precarious for supporters of the CPDM including the much respected fons of the North West Province. Hostile incidents against chiefs were registered in several parts of the province although none was directed at Ganyonga. In Mankon for example, fon Angwafor was confronted by accusations and threats from his subjects who blacklisted him for complicity with the CPDM administration. These accusations became more grievous during the state of emergency, when on 3 November 1992, hundreds of subjects stormed his palace to protest against his 'meddling' in partisan politics. Desperate to register their disillusion unidentified protesters also burnt down his rest house in Bamenda.

[68]

Elsewhere in the chiefdom of Ndu, soldiers and members of the gendarmerie shot and killed six citizens protesting against the supposedly stolen victory. The fon's silence over the matter provoked the subjects to accuse him of collaborating with the CPDM and of being an auxiliary of state repression. Thereafter, subjects began to denounce him publicly and others called him by his name which was interpreted as an open sign of dethronement (Fisiy 1995:55).

According to several schools of thought, the enthusiasm for democratic change in Cameroon was a short-lived experience. Advocates of this view hold that such enthusiasm petered out 'shortly after the presidential elections of October 1992, when the public was made to understand that democracy is not necessarily having as president the person the majority wants' (Nyamnjoh, 1999:114). But this disillusion also intensified resentment against the CPDM and its local supporters, especially in the Bamenda grasslands where the SDF continued to maintain its dominance over other political parties.

This was evident in the first local government election of January 1996. The election coincided with the promulgation of the revised 1972 Constitution which increased the presidential term to a maximum of two terms consisting of seven years each.[58] Be that as it may, the local council election of 1996 was very significant because of the victory registered by the SDF in many municipalities of the North West Province.

Ganyonga sought to make use of this opportunity to head the local council by declaring his candidature in the CPDM in for Bali. It was not a strange idea for a fon to head the local council. In fact, Fonyonga II had headed the Bali Native Authority during his tenure as fon of Bali. More recently, Galega II had led the local council in the 1960s.[59] Many subjects were against the idea of the fon competing for political office against another subject. Informants insisted that it was not 'proper' for the fon to compete with a commoner in democratic elections, because if the fon were defeated it would bring dishonour and shame to his status. This view was particularly prominent among CPDM militants. In general, the subjects resented the idea of the fon participating overtly in party politics. According to them, although the fon had a democratic right to be involved in partisan politics and to vote for a party of his choice, his overt participation had the risk of ruining his relationship with subjects who supported opposition parties.

What is more, even some members of the CPDM were against the fact that Ganyonga should stand as the party candidate for the election. The fon's determination to run for the post led to chaos within the CPDM constituency of Bali. CPDM militants who opposed his candidature decided to elect their own candidate, excluding the fon. Eventually the CPDM had two contenders for the post of mayor within the same municipality, the fon and a rival subject. Although the fon emerged as the CPDM candidate, in the end he was defeated by the opposition SDF.[60] His defeat made him very unpopular as predicted by those who opposed his running for the mayoral office.

After their victory, the local SDF leadership in Bali resolved to visit the fon ostensibly to reassure him of their unalloyed loyalty. Although this was the official policy of the SDF, many of its militants decided instead to celebrate the fon's humiliation at the palace ground, much to his displeasure. Other subjects who were opposed to the fon's 'meddling' in party politics began to disobey instructions from the palace as a way of registering their disappointment with the fon. At a particular period, some informants claimed, people refused to provide free labour to the fon, provoking him to place a temporary ban on all *death celebrations*[61] (cry-die) until subjects complied with his demands. Ardent supporters of the fon insisted that subjects who failed to provide their labour to the fon did so, not out of political differences or resentment against the fon but because those in charge of organising such activities failed to do their job properly.[62]

The fon's humiliation at the polls in 1996 is still remembered with much indignation. Although the fon has not dared to run for political office after 1996, he has nonetheless, remained deeply involved in CPDM and chiefdom politics. This has triggered a major debate about the role of chiefs in the democratic era. The two main positions are on the one hand, the view that chiefs should actively participate in party politics and on the other, that they should maintain a neutral role.

I begin by exploring some of the specific claims made by the fon and his collaborators on this matter. Besides the fact that it was his constitutional right to be a card-carrying member of any political party of his choice, the fon maintained that he chose the ruling CPDM in order to attract development to his chiefdom. Although he had his own personal interests to protect, he argued repeatedly that given the 'complex' nature of politics in Cameroon (referring to the false democratic context) he was better positioned to protect the interests of his people by siding with the ruling party rather than with an opposition party such as the SDF that was unlikely to win power in the near future. According to him, it was worthless to sow where one was not sure to reap.[63] This view was not unique to Ganyonga granting that several chiefs have adopted similar positions in regard to their involvement in party politics on the side of the ruling party.

Despite this controversial stand, Ganyonga had a few sympathisers. An informant maintained that the fon had a responsibility to support the ruling party/government because he benefited in many ways from it. As an auxiliary of the government, it was incumbent on him to be obedient and supportive of the party and government policies. In a patronage system such as Cameroon's, the informant observed, the fon owed his job as a lecturer to the Biya government. According to a popular saying, the fon could not dare to bite the finger that fed him. This was because he also received payment from the government as an 'auxiliary of the administration'. Furthermore, the fact that he was a board member of MIDENO (a government development agency for the North West Province) implied that he ought to show allegiance to the CPDM government.

The above notwithstanding, a majority of informants resented the fon's overt partisanship. He was accused of showing 'excessive' support for the ruling party and condemned his tendency to politicise every event in the chiefdom. Many informants contended that he seemed to be 'overdoing' it – that is, politicising his interactions with subjects. The women of Etoma I (a quarter in Bali), for example, expressed their disapproval of the fon's attempt to woo them to the CPDM during their visit to the palace to present a newly established women's 'common initiative' association. To their dismay, the women alleged, the fon ignored what they had come for, and instead reminded them of their obligation to follow wherever he led them, because, as their father, he could not mislead them. The women left the palace discontented while some vowed never to set foot on the palace again.

Youths expressed similar bitterness towards him after a visit to the palace. In 2000 a group of youths who had won a football trophy organised by the Bali Nyonga Development and Cultural Association (BANDECA) visited the palace to present their prize to the fon. After congratulating them on their victory, the fon remarked that he could not wait to see what they would do to bring victory to the CPDM in Bali during forthcoming elections. He was referring specifically to the council election that was scheduled for 2001. Although the election was postponed several times by the Biya government, it finally took place on 30 June 2002. Despite the supposed massive irregularities that marred the election throughout the country, the SDF won the local government seat in Bali. Its major rival was the CPDM whose candidate was a Yaounde-based government elite. He was also the national president of BANDECA, an elite association whose activities will be discussed shortly.

Many of those who objected to the fon's participation in party politics did so from a perspective of custom or tradition. According to them, it was 'uncustomary' for fons to compete for political positions with commoners because, as it were, the fon was 'above' party politics – he was the father of all subjects, regardless of which political party his subjects supported.[64] An informant drew a distinction between politics in traditional society and politics in the modern state and concluded that in modern politics, there was little or no respect for tradition or one's status:

Chiefs should not participate in party politics because modern politics is a dirty game. Tradition demands that we should respect our fon, but in politics, there is no respect for a person's status or title, so it is not fair for commoners to address the chief in a similar way they would another subject. I have seen common people speaking to our fon carelessly and some even insulted him in the face just because of politics.[65]

Others objected to the fon's partisanship on the grounds that the political field was impermanent, given that competition for power was a continuous process. One informant wondered about the fate of fons who supported the ruling party and their chances of survival if the ruling party lost elections or was replaced at the national level. This, he argued, would bring a lot of dishonour and ridicule to the fon. He was referring to Ganyonga's defeat in the local council election of 1996 by the SDF, which remains very popular in Bali.

Over the years the political climate in Cameroon has changed especially in reference to the people' expectations about democracy since the early 1990s. After the 1997 presidential election, boycotted by the SDF, it began to dawn on civil society that the SDF`s chances of taking over power in the near future were slim. The SDF seems to be experiencing diminishing returns due to several factors, one of them being its unclear position regarding the Anglophone problem, which has gained more popularity in recent years.[66]

The SDF's dwindling fortunes can be illustrated best by the parliamentary/local council elections of July 2007 in which it won only 14 seats, having lost over 50% of the seats it held between 1997 and 2006. On the contrary, the CPDM now holds over 90% of the seats in parliament, more than it has ever had since the re-introduction of multiparty politics. Of course, there is strong evidence that the CPDM government has regained its dominance over the years thanks to sophisticated rigging instruments and disrespect of the democratic norms that govern elections (see for instance, the Amnesty International Report for Cameroon 2005).[67]

This means that chiefs who either had sympathy for the opposition or espoused neutrality as their political gospel have gradually renounced such positions and opted for the CPDM. An example is the fon of Nso, Mbinglo III who gave up his so-called 'neutrality' and 'officially' joined the CPDM in April 2001. On his accession to the throne, Mbinglo III followed the example of his late father by addressing a letter to all the subjects of Nso in which he expressed his neutrality and commitment to a non-partisan chieftainship.

> I wish to state emphatically that, so far as party politics are concerned, I shall follow the strategy of functioning as an 'umbrella' to all the sons and daughters of Nso, irrespective of the political party to which they may belong. I shall not participate in party activities such as election campaign rallies organised by any political party. (*Cameroon Post* No. 0191 Wednesday, November 24 - December 1 1993, pg.2)

In Bali, more people are becoming less hostile to the fon's involvement in CPDM politics although this should not be mistaken for their acceptance of his claim to legitimacy in this respect. On the contrary, the masses seem more preoccupied with the 'Anglophone problem' (discussed below) which continues to gather momentum, especially with the failure of the SDF to capture power. It is partly because of the fon's pronouncement and actions on the Anglophone issue in the 1990s that he has won some degree of legitimacy in the eyes of his people. His involvement in specific lobbies also helped to dilute the low esteem the people had for him. However his role on issues such as the 'water crisis' (discussed below) revived suspicion and resentment against him for a while. In the following paragraphs, I will consider the fon's role in each of these different issues and assess the extent to which he gained or lost popularity.

Ganyonga was at the helm of a lobby which advocated the elevation of the chiefdom from a sub-division under Mezam division to a fully fledged administrative division. In fact, during fieldwork for this project it was rumoured that President Paul Biya had already signed a decree for the establishment of the division but had suspended it due to opposition from neighbouring Meta chiefs and notables who accused the Bali fon of nursing expansionist ambitions.[68] The fon and key members of the CPDM in the chiefdom have emphasised the need for the Bali population to show their support to the CPDM government in order to hasten the establishment of the division. According to them, government will delay the process if Bali continues to remain a stronghold of the SDF. Although this was the case, the fon and his notables pointed to the fact that the government had already established a new Government Technical High School and a *Gendarmerie Compagnie* in Bali. This was evidence, the notables pointed out, that the Bali Division was in the process of being established since the above-named institutions were found only at divisional headquarters, not in sub-divisions. If the division was created, the fon and his collaborators observed, the chiefdom would attract more socio-economic development in the form of more schools, jobs, hospitals, and better roads. However, many informants were sceptical about the extent to which their lives would change as a result of the elevation of the sub-division to a division. Some cynics pointed out that the reconfiguration of the area into a division was intended to bring repression nearer to the people, not development.

The fon was also behind the struggle to regain Bali's status as a parliamentary constituency. This particular issue needs a brief historical background. Before the parliamentary election of 1997, the Biya government re-designed the 180 parliamentary constituencies in the country. Although this is not obvious, the logic was to place constituencies away from possible SDF strongholds to areas where the CPDM was likely to win. Given the popularity of the SDF in Bali as demonstrated in the council election of 1996, the Bali constituency was combined with Santa, a neighbouring chiefdom. It was anticipated that the CPDM would win the Bali-Santa seat because the former Prime Minister, Achidi Achu originated from the Santa sub-division. Eventually the SDF won the seat despite desperate attempts by the local CPDM elite to win the seat for the CPDM. This failure on their part triggered renewed hope among the fon and elite in Bali that the chiefdom could regain its previous status as a single constituency. This discourse was also connected to the lobby for a fully fledged administrative division. While the fon and some CPDM elite were preoccupied with these issues, many subjects on the contrary, did not mind whether Bali or Santa was the elected parliamentary constituency. In fact many informants contended that although the former SDF parliamentarian (1997-2007) was not a subject of Bali, he made more substantial contributions to the Bali sub-division than a Bali subject had done between 1992 and 1997 as a CPDM parliamentarian.

Another domain in which fon Ganyonga sought to win legitimacy was in maintaining his hegemony in the region and protecting the borders of the chiefdom from other neighbouring chiefs who were making claims on Bali territory. It was also alleged that two non-Bali villages that were previously under the control of Ganyonga had recently obtained their autonomy. This was interpreted by the subjects as a sign of weakness on Ganyonga's part. In 1995 Bali had a skirmish with the neighbouring chiefdom of Chomba over a border dispute. It was believed that the Chomba fighters had received financial and material support from some CPDM elite of their chiefdom.[69] While these disputes became more frequent, some notables argued that Bali was not 'CPDM-enough' to be protected by the government. According to them, this meant that the state has sided with smaller chiefdoms against Bali due to the popular support enjoyed by the SDF in the chiefdom.

Almost every contentious issue in Bali could be explained in terms of party politics. Apparently, the 'demons' were CPDM militants while the 'saints' were depicted as SDF. This dichotomy was illustrated by the struggle over the management of water supply in the chiefdom. During the period of my fieldwork, Bali was in a state of serious water crisis. It was alleged that a change in the management of the Bali Community Water Committee (BCWC) was partly to blame. According to informants, the hidden hands of certain CPDM elite and the fon in particular were behind the crisis. The previous management, led by a non-partisan notable and retired CDC worker was replaced by a leading member of the CPDM in Bali. When the water crisis eventually started, it was rumoured that the crisis was a deliberate attempt by the new management to hand over the water supply to the National Water Corporation

(SNEC) in return for 15 million CFA Francs. In order to understand the complex nature of the crisis, a brief background to the story of water supply in Bali is needed.

The Bali water system was built in 1957 during the British colonial administration and was administered by the Bali Native Authority under the leadership of fon Galega II. This remained so after independence until the management was taken over by the state monopoly, SNEC. It is uncertain at what point SNEC took over the management, although it was apparent that its management was inefficient and unpopular in the chiefdom. In the early 1990s people complained of high bills and untreated water, and sometimes water was unavailable for several days. The Bali Rural Council also complained of SNEC's threats to cut water supply in the town because of unpaid bills amounting to 17 million CFA Francs. The last straw to break the camel's back was SNEC's decision to cut the water supply to the palace, an action that provoked the anger of the Bali population against SNEC. On 10 January 1994, the population of Bali stormed the local SNEC office and ordered the officials out of the town after demanding that their water installations should be handed over to local management. The office was also set ablaze and most of the SNEC documents and bills destroyed.

After the successful overthrow of SNEC, the Bali Community Water Committee (BCWC) was established as a management committee to oversee the functioning of the installations. Bills were reduced significantly and Bali elites in Cameroon and abroad were requested to make annual contributions to ensure the smooth operation of the water supply. In 1996, Bali elites in the United States, under the banner of the Bali Cultural Association - USA (BCA-USA), established a Water Committee which devised a plan through which members could make contributions and pay the bills of their families back in Bali.[70] The BCWC functioned without any major crisis from 1994 to 2000.

It is claimed, however, that before the Water Committee was established, the fon had expressed desire to head the Committee. But Bali elites had opposed the fon's wishes and advocated instead for a commoner to be elected who would be accountable to the fon and the population. As a result, the fon is reported to have withdrawn his candidature leading to the election of a notable, Mr. Babila, to head the water committee.

In 2000, the leadership of the water committee was changed following an election that was generally perceived to be dubious. Mr Billa, another notable and prominent member of the CPDM, took up leadership of the committee. According to informants, it was rumoured that the government had promised to reward the fon and Mr Billa with the sum of 15 million CFA Francs if they returned the water supply to SNEC. In line with the speculation, it was alleged that the poor management of the water supply was the committee's ploy to attract government intervention with the intent of taking over control of the water installations. Mr Billa rejected the rumours as baseless and explained that the installations were old and needed to be replaced. Sceptics insisted that he was not devoted to the management of the water system and lacked the expertise or experience required for such technicla matters. Mr Babila was hailed as a man who had devoted all his time to ensure that the Bali population had a regular flow of water. Although the water crisis has been partially resolved, it remains a contentious issue and continues to be politicised despite evidence that the rumours were ill-founded.

Although Ganyonga has not founded his own development trust like Chief Tshivhase in Venda, he took keen interest in the development initiatives of his subjects. It was in this particular domain that informants spoke positively about the chief. Ganyonga was involved in the activities of the Bali Nyonga Development and Cultural Association (BANDECA), an elite group consisting of civil servants and business persons interested in the socio-economic development of the chiefdom. Most of the members were migrants who resided in other towns and cities of Cameroon, but maintained strong links with the chiefdom. Some of the members intend to settle in Bali upon retirement from the civil service or business. Because of its 'translocal' nature, the association had regional branches in the major towns and cities of Cameroon such as Yaounde, Douala, Limbe, Bamenda and Kumba.

The association took over from the defunct Bali Social, Cultural and Development Association (BASCUDA) in the 1990s but soon became moribund itself. It was revived in 1999 and eventually resumed its activities in 2000. Its formal operations began on 20 December 1999 during a function where the fon installed the new executive in the presence of the mayor and the sub divisional officer of Bali. Since its revival, BANDECA has successfully raised more than 20 million CFA Francs.[71] It has also set up a community library, built a modern urinal and bathroom at the town centre and donated computers to Government High School Bali and medical equipment to the District Hospital. Bali immigrants in the US have also assisted BANDECA by starting a programme to provide scholarships to promising students of Bali origin, aimed at improving the educational standards in the chiefdom. Bali subjects in the UK have donated equipment and motor bikes to the association to assist with transportation costs.

Figure 5: Motorbikes donated to BANDECA by Bali immigrants in the UK.
Photo courtesy of <u>mbonbani@yahoogroups.com</u>

The fon has visited the main branches of the association to encourage and demonstrate his commitment to the cause of the elite.[72] While many informants were impressed with the fon's involvement in BANDECA initiatives, they are yet to endorse his claims to participation in modern politics.

Ganyonga and Chiefs' Politics in the Democratic Era

One of the ways in which fons in the grassfields tried to boost their claim to legitimacy in the democratic era was by creating elite associations to address their collective interests. Secondary sources reveal that Ganyonga played an influential role at particular instances during the formation of fons' organisations. This process began in April 1993 when traditional rulers in the North West Province met at the fon's palace in the chiefdom of Nkwen to establish the North West Fons Association (NOWEFA) led by fon Fosi Yakum-taw, a former governor of the North Province. Fon Ganyonga was elected as the Secretary General of the association. The newly created body had the primary objective of encouraging mutual coexistence among the fons and their chiefdoms and to lobby development aid to their respective chiefdoms in particular and the North West Province in general. The fons also declared the neutrality of the association with respect to multiparty politics even though some members insisted that the association should declare its support for the ruling CPDM of which several of them were not only members but also office holders.[73]

It did not take long for the hidden hand of the CPDM to betray itself as an influential factor in chiefs' affairs. In August 1995 the fon of Balikumbat with the alleged complicity of the then Prime Minister, Achidi Achu, created the North West Fons Conference (NOWEFCO) as an alternative to NOWEFA. The new association sought to unite fons who were members of the CPDM with the intention of publicly declaring their support for the ruling party (cf. Nyamnjoh and Rowlands 1998). This was clearly opposed to NOWEFA's policy of neutrality. As soon as it emerged that Achidi Achu was behind this new association, Ganyonga is reported to have publicly accused him of being a traitor: 'we the fons now look upon the Prime Minister with disdain, as a traitor among the fons of the North West Province.'[74]

The split among the fons was also interpreted as an expression of the on-going contest between 'first class' and non-first class fons. Although NOWEFA was made up of non-first class fons, it was dominated by the first class chiefs of the grassfields, while NOWEFCO consisted of the majority of second and third class chiefs. Actually, in terms of numbers, NOWEFCO claimed to have 200 of the 230 chiefs in the North West Province. Its leader, fon Doh Gah Gwanyin of Bali Kumbat, argued further that: 'all fondoms are autonomous and equal. No fondom is superior to the other, neither is there any fondom which is equal to 20 fondoms.'[75] This declaration confirmed the suspicion among observers that the major dividing line between the two associations was the distinction and prestige accorded to particular fons and not to others. NOWEFCO's leader was not the only one opposed to the distinction of chiefs into classes of prestige and power. The SDF leader, John Fru Ndi spoke out against the categorisation of traditional leaders: 'A fon is a fon. No first-class or third-class fons exist in the North West, except creations to split and retard the province.'[76]

[76]

While a majority of the first class chiefs maintained that NOWEFA was the only legitimate fons' association in the province, fon Angwafor III of Mankon, a prominent member of the CPDM opted to recognise and support the rival association, NOWEFCO. This triggered calls for the dissolution of the two associations and the formation of a new and inclusive association. A few opinion leaders argued against a single association for chiefs and that such thinking was reminiscent of the one-party era. An SDF parliamentarian for example argued that chiefs needed to have several associations reflecting the spirit of multiparty democracy: 'since multipartyism means the blossoming of various shades of opinion that must not necessarily come from one side, there is a need for many fons' associations provided they are ... for the interest of their fondoms.'[77]

In May 1998 the fons held a 'union' meeting at the fon of Nkwen's palace purportedly to unite the two factions. NOWEFCO's leader boycotted the union meeting but a significant number of its members attended. Also present at the meeting were fons Angwafor of Mankon, Ganyonga of Bali and Mbinglo of Nso. At this crucial meeting, the two associations were allegedly dissolved and the North West Fons Union (NOWEFU) created headed by fon Abumbi II of Bafut – a first class chief. As soon the new association came into existence, Achidi Achu, who was partly to blame for the division among the fons, accompanied a delegation to the Prime Minister's office in June 1998 to lobby for the recognition of the newly created NOWEFU. Reports claim that the then Prime Minister, Peter Musonge (who succeeded Achidi Achu in 1997) was not pleased because the new association had failed to express a 'motion of support' for the CPDM administration, given the fact that he had contributed 2 million CFA Francs for the organisation of the meeting.[78] This, according to him, confirmed the claims of fon Doh Gah Gwanyin, the NOWEFCO leader that the new association was a pro-opposition group. Since its formation, fon Doh, a diehard member of the CPDM has held on to his own faction despite its feeble presence in the landscape of chiefs' politics in the North West Province. In fact, NOWEFU has increasingly alienated fon Doh from their association, desperate to rehabilitate their image as friendly to the democratic dispensation, unlike fon Doh known for his speedy resort to violence against opponents. In February 2005, the Cameroon National Assembly lifted fon Doh of his parliamentary immunity, paving the way for him to stand trial on murder charges with respect to the death of John Kohtem, SDF district chairman of the Ngohketunjia division (within which Bali Kumbat is located).[79] Fon Doh was eventually found guilty and sentenced to 15 years imprisonment for masterminding and participating in the murder of the SDF district chairman – who incidentally was also his brother-in-law. [80] News of his demise was received with unprecedented jubilation particularly in opposition circles and even among his own subjects. Recent developments indicate that celebration among fon Doh's opponents was premature because he now lives as a free man, having served only a few months in jail – buttressed by the statements of the Minister of Justice in the National Assembly that Fon Doh was a non-convict.[81]

It is unlikely that unity will be achieved, given the infighting among chiefs in NOWEFU as well as the rogue status of Chief Doh. Recent crisis has rocked NOWEFU following a series of personal conflicts between the NOWEFU president fon Chafah (a Magistrate) and Nico Halle (a prominent barrister) and current NOWEFU *ntumfor* or spokesperson– translated as 'the fon's mouthpiece').[82] This crisis was deepened in late August 2008 when NOWEFU President, fon Chafah unilaterally suspended the ntumfor from his position without consulting his colleagues.[83] NOWEFU's Secretary General has publicly challenged the legality of the president's action whilst other chiefs have expressed disdain over the president's controversial actions.[84]

Despite the challenges they face, the fons individually and as members of groups have negotiated their status within the patron-client networks of Cameroon's bureaucratic order by lobbying for government positions.[85] Some have even called for the re-establishment of the House of Chiefs. Chiefs have also found fresh use for traditional titles, which they have awarded to government elite, aimed at penetrating state circles.[86] New chiefs' associations at divisional levels have also emerged which aim to further the socio-economic development of their administrative divisions while complementing the broader aims of NOWEFU – (for example, the Ngoketunjia Fon's Union visited the Prime Minister's office in September 2008 and called on the national government to create a state university in the North West Province and to pave some of the roads in their division).

Through these associations, chiefs have made claims to local authority and have competed for recognition even against each other, aimed at positioning themselves in the best possible way within the corridors of state power. In a context where the politics of recognition is rife, chiefs supporting the ruling CPDM have claimed to be the true representatives of their regions or chiefdoms by lobbying for development in compensation for their support to the ruling party. But not all chiefs have been successful to the same degree. Some are more prominent and/or popular than others. In the next section, I will show how Ganyonga in particular has won some measure of legitimacy on account of his involvement in the so-called 'Anglophone problem'.

Ganyonga and the Anglophone Problem

In the preceding chapter I argued that political liberalisation provided room for the expression of perceived or actual injustices by individuals and communities that had been reluctant to do so during the authoritarian period. One of the issues that arose from the new democratic dispensation was the rise in Anglophone activism and protest against Francophone domination as well as demands for the reconfiguration of state power (Konings and Nyamnjoh 2003). Since 1990 traditional rulers of the grassfields have been very vocal about the plight of the English-speaking minority in Cameroon. Of these chiefs, fon Ganyonga has probably been most prominent – at least in 1990s given that his public position on this issue has changed during the last eight years. In this section, I will show Ganyonga's involvement, together with other fons of the grassfields in articulating the concerns of their subjects.

The Anglophone problem became popular after the first *All Anglophone Conference* (AACI) which took place in Buea (the capital of the former Southern Cameroons) on the 2nd and 3rd of April 1993 (Konings and Nyamnjoh 1997). Ganyonga not only led the delegation of North West fons to this important event, he also served as one of the secretaries at the conference. The outcome of the conference was the Buea Declaration,[87] which denounced the 'assimilationist tendency' of the Francophone-dominated state and the marginalisation of English-speaking citizens. The Declaration was widely welcomed among the Anglophone community although the South West Chiefs' Conference condemned it. North West fons, on the contrary, applauded it as a major step towards debate for a better Cameroon.

During the conference, the fons addressed the 5000 conference participants. Among other things, they called for the reinstatement of the House of Chiefs abolished in 1972 'to ensure the active participation of Traditional rulers in decision-making on matters of national importance. That a Federal system of Government be re-instituted, taking cognisance of our Colonial and Cultural heritage. That the Minority rights of the Anglophone Cameroonians be clearly protected and anchored in the Constitution.'[88]

When the fons returned to Bamenda, they met at the chief's palace in Nkwen on April 25 1993 and voted overwhelmingly in favour of the Buea Declaration despite Prime Minister Achidi Achu's attempts to dissuade them.[89] In a follow-up address to the visiting Secretary General of the Commonwealth in June 1993, fon Ganyonga III of Bali and several elites of the province argued against the admission of Cameroon into the Commonwealth on the grounds that the government had not met the requirements of the Harare declaration. They insisted that:

> The Commonwealth needs to be informed that the Anglophones are the main victims of human rights abuses in Cameroon, and that they are the target group of the policy of assimilation into French culture (a process which in present day Cameroon is given that pleasant label of 'National Integration'). The admission of Cameroon to membership of the Commonwealth now, will amount to an endorsement of the policy of assimilation being pursued by the Francophone led governments of this country since 1972.[90]

Despite his membership and prominence in the CPDM, Ganyonga was acclaimed for his public pronouncements in favour of the Anglophone cause. During a visit to the fon's palace by the SDF leader, John Fru Ndi, the fon argued that 'Cameroon is not for any one person or for any group of people. This country belongs to us all, and we have a right to be here. We (Anglophones) cannot be second-class citizens in our own country.'

Although most fons did not attend the second All Anglophone Conference (AACII) held in Bamenda in 1994 (probably due to government pressure to boycott), the fons still voiced their opinion on important issues affecting the anglophone community. At the Bamenda conference, a Southern Cameroons National Council (SCNC) was established to lobby the government of Cameroon and the international community for more constitutional recognition of Anglophone rights. Following the SCNC's historic trip to the United Nations in 1995, calls for the recognition of an Anglophone identity and rights reached fever pitch. Fon Fosi Yakum-taw, a former Governor of the North Province, called on the government to address the Anglophone problem before it escalated into severe conflict:

> if we as traditional rulers find that a certain shade of opinion is pressing and gaining grounds, it is our role to invite government to listen to them. We have not said government must accept or refuse but that government should enter into dialogue instead of just ignoring the existence of certain people or certain issues. Government ought to examine these problems and convince people that these problems don't exist or recognise the problems. Government has so far been

talking about unity, about peace and progress. We think government itself should open and talk to the SCNC with a view to preserving the peace and unity of this nation which we as traditional rulers, we as custodians of traditional rights and liberties, see somehow threatened and we think that government ought to initiate action as quickly as possible.[91]

Despite the campaign by lobby groups Cameroon was admitted to the Commonwealth on 16 October 1995. This was a serious setback for Anglophone activists, especially the SCNC. Gradually the SCNC receded into oblivion, mainly because of the local government and parliamentary elections that dominated the political scene in 1996 and 1997 respectively. Meanwhile the SCNC changed its status from a pressure group to what appeared as a "nationalist" movement, causing many chiefs to dissociate themselves from its activities.

On 31st December 1999 the SCNC, led by retired justice, Alobwede Ebong seized the government-controlled Radio station in Buea and declared the independence of the Southern Cameroons. They were subsequently arrested and jailed, provoking further calls for Anglophone nationalism. Most chiefs joined government officials to condemn SCNC activities, especially on October 1 2001 when the movement celebrated Independence Day leading to confrontation with state security forces and the consequent killing of three persons. Despite their differences, prominent chiefs are still vocal about the plight of the Anglophone community. During the installation of a government minister of North West origin in 2002, fon Angwafor III of Mankon used the occasion to call on Paul Biya to 'open a university in the North West, tar the ring road and solve the Anglophone problem...'[92]

Although fon Ganyonga had been an ardent Anglophone activist, many informants were of the opinion that he seemed to have given up the 'fight'. Informants were displeased that he had joined other fons to condemn SCNC celebrations on 1 October 2001. It should be pointed out that some of the prominent members of the SCNC are Bali subjects and consequently command a huge following in Bali and the North West Province in general. Some informants held that the fon is still supportive of the Anglophone cause but had decided not to publicise his opinion on the matter.

On 1 October 2002, the government deployed heavily armed soldiers to Bamenda, the capital of the North West province to pre-empt what it perceived as a secessionist attempt by the Anglophones. The Anglophone population held that they were celebrating 41 years of their independence from British rule. According to local accounts and press releases from the SCNC leadership, the police and Gendarmes arrested more than 25 people at the celebration grounds in Bamenda. They also tortured and intimidated citizens in some parts of the city, with the intention of deterring citizens from taking part in the ceremonies.[93]

Given the resurgence of the SCNC and its dominant role in the political activities of the North West Province, the chiefs have decided to join the bandwagon to advocate a solution to the Anglophone problem. Contrary to the position adopted by most chiefs before and after the 1 October celebrations in 2001, the chiefs have become more vocal about the plight of their people and the Anglophone minority as a whole. On 19 October 2002 fon Ganyonga and several first class fons of the North West Province made a trip to the presidency in Yaounde to present a memorandum on the Anglophone problem and the 'underdevelopment' of the North West province in particular.[94] The trip was highly acclaimed by both their subjects and the Anglophone press. The *Herald* for example referred to the trip as 'a commendable act of leadership'[95] and urged Anglophone parliamentarians to emulate the fons by organising forums through which the Anglophone problem could be articulated and acted upon.

Ganyonga and Public Opinion

Thus far, this chapter has described and analysed the kinds of legitimacy claimed by Ganyonga in the democratic era and the extent to which his subjects have accepted, contested or rejected such claims. The main finding is that although Ganyonga is prominent in national politics, his claims to legitimacy in the politics of the democratic era have been seriously contested. His involvement on the side of the ruling party is perceived by the people as a failure on his part to provide a shield for them against the predation of the state. But Ganyonga's status is ambivalent. On the one hand, he is seen to be on the side of the state and on the other, he seems to have been prominent among fons in expressing the cause of the oppressed Anglophone minority. This explains the ambiguity of opinions about the fon. In this section, I examine how Ganyonga's decisions on local political issues have affected his relationship with his subjects. Opinions about the fon are categorised into two principal domains: his involvement in partisan politics and perceptions about his leadership styles insofar as traditional government is concerned.

When I began fieldwork for this book in early December 2001, there was widespread concern about the fon's long and unusual absence from the chiefdom. This was during the Lela[96] season, a period of thanksgiving, celebration and merriment cherished dearly by the people. Everywhere in the chiefdom, women, men and youths were busy preparing for the great annual festival. A new fence had been erected on all sides of the fon's palace, perceived as an indication of the impending festival. Informants insisted that the fon had expressed certainty that the festival would take place. But news began to circulate that he had travelled out of the country and may not return in time for the festival. Many did not know his specific whereabouts, but it was rumoured that he had travelled to visit his family in Germany. Despite his absence, people continued with preparations, hopeful that that the fon would return in time to preside over the festival.

At the end of December the fon had not yet returned, provoking considerable disappointment among the masses. I was also beginning to lose patience, trying to come to terms with the fact that I had lost my first opportunity of participating in the Lela festival. Had he known he would not be around, many suggested, he should not have permitted them to prepare for the festival. This was proof, his detractors argued, that the fon was not particularly interested in local affairs. People who had travelled from the cities to attend the festival also felt betrayed by the fon. Eventually, rumour began to circulate in mid-February 2002 that he was back in town.

Many informants resented the fact that the fon was involved in partisan politics. I have already described the different views about the fon's involvement on this matter. However, there was a general feeling that the fon had extended his partisan politics to the affairs of traditional government. Notables, especially those of the SDF alleged that the fon had marginalized people who did not belong to his party thus turning the traditional council[97] into a puppet institution. My discussion with several traditional councillors confirmed these allegations. In my interview with the vice-chairman of the traditional council, for example, he insisted that the traditional council's role was not to contest or check the fon's powers but to facilitate and collaborate with him. In his opinion, members of the traditional council should support the fon's party. To emphasise his point, he repeatedly asked: 'how do you expect the fon to bring people into the council that he doesn't trust?' [98] Some of the notables who felt sidelined stated that they had stopped going to the palace as an expression of their disillusionment with the way things were being run in the chiefdom.

Notwithstanding the above, many women were delighted with the fon's appointment of a woman into the traditional council, the first of its kind in the history of area:

> We support the fon as part of our duty to uphold our tradition. That is why the fon saw the necessity to appoint a woman into the traditional council in recognition of the role we have played in this chiefdom. Women now have a say in the affairs of the traditional council.[99]

Although this was commended as a positive development, some women argued that a single female representative was insufficient.

The fon was also unpopular due to allegations that he had devalued the status of traditional titles in the chiefdom. Whilst several informants accused the fon of trading the titles for economic gains, others argued that he was simply trying to adapt tradition to modern demands. In Bali, the status of *nkom* (pl. *kom*) was the highest to which a male commoner could aspire. In the past, the title was awarded to persons of substance during the Lela festival, especially to those who had distinguished themselves in local crafts or in battle. Today it is awarded to bureaucratic and party elite or members of the chiefdom who have made substantial contributions to the community. The title does not give them legislative or executive functions but they form a sort of informal senate which may or may not be consulted by the fon as his inclinations dictate. Except for the seven permanent *kom* that existed when the chiefdom was founded, the title of *nkom* was usually non-hereditary. This means that aspirants were expected to earn their titles. As a mark of distinction the *nkom* was given a red feather often worn on a woven cap.

Many informants were unhappy about the growing number of *kom* members in the chiefdom and some accused the fon of devaluing the prestige linked to the title. Some key informants held that Ganyonga once awarded three titles at a single Lela festival, whereas his father had often let a festival go by without giving any award. Others pointed out that the growing number of title-holders was in proportion to the increase in population. Those who complained, I was told, were probably envious individuals who had failed to attract recognition, if at all, they had worthy achievements to their names.

The fon also became unpopular for acting in what was described as an 'unfatherly' manner against a bereaved family and for ordering the exhumation of the corpse of the deceased family head. In August 1996, the Musong family sued the fon for 'disturbance of quiet enjoyment of premises, theft, invasion of residence, threats to lives, illegal exhumation and desecration and reburial of ...(their)...father's corpse.'[100] The story goes that the late Musong and his family lived on his property a few metres away from the fon's palace. During the reign of the former chief, Galega II, a dispute had emerged over the ownership of the land and Musong had won a lawsuit against the fon. However, the present fon contested the legality of Musong's claim and appealed against the court judgement by arguing that the disputed land was part of royal territory on which Mr Musong's forebears had settled illegally. When Musong died in August 1996, his family defied the fon's injunction not to bury the deceased on the disputed land. A couple of hours after the burial, the *mupuh* (the traditional police) arrived and ordered the family to evacuate the land in less than half an hour. Unable to pack up their personal effects within the stipulated time, the family was forced to leave many of their belongings behind. These allegedly became the property of the fon according to 'custom'. The *mupuh* proceeded to exhume the corpse of the late Musong and buried him elsewhere without the knowledge of the Musong family. In the lawsuit filed by Barrister Bobga, the Musong family charged the fon and six others for illegally exhuming the corpse of their father and forcefully evicting them from their property.

The fon was found guilty and ordered to pay for damages. Meanwhile those who were responsible for the actual exhumation were given prison sentences of three months each. This event brought the traditional police into disrepute. It also made the fon even more unpopular among his subjects who felt that the prison sentences delivered to the *mupuh* were symbolically directed to him. Just like the fon's defeat at the polls in that same year, this incident is still fresh in the minds of those who oppose his leadership style.

The above evidence confirms Fisiy's (1995) and Nyamnjoh's (2002) studies in different chiefdoms in the grassfields of Cameroon. Fisiy's work was preoccupied with showing the ways in which chiefs sought to legitimise their participation in Cameroon's democratic transition. His main finding was that although many chiefs had become quite unpopular for siding with the CPDM, they had designed new ways of securing their influence and power through the 'control and management of land.' By demarcating a political space (land) within which they could maintain their control over people and resources, chiefs were able to contest the postcolonial terrain and lay claim to local power. Fon Ganyonga of Bali has been involved in similar kinds of claims. Although his reputation was brought to question due to his desire to manage strategic resources such as water, he has focussed on maintaining the territorial integrity of his chiefdom against land claims made by neighbouring Meta chiefs and recently by the Bawock. Lobbying for his chiefdom to be elevated to the level of a division is also indicative of his desire to lay claim to local authority.

Nyamnjoh's main thesis is that chieftaincy is a dynamic institution and that chiefs should be seen as agents in their own right. According to him, chieftaincy needs to be 'understood not only, and not even primarily, as belonging to a pre-modern, pre-capitalist past; but rather as institutions which have either (been) adapted to the contemporary socio-political setting, or even have been specifically created for or by it' (Harneit-Sievers 1998:57 cited in Nyamnjoh 2002:4). Against this background, Nyamnjoh contends that chiefs' claims to legitimacy in the democratic era in Cameroon can be 'determined by anticipation and recognition of or failure to attract state-driven development efforts in their chiefdoms' (ibid. 14). Taking this view into account, this research shows that although Ganyonga has failed to persuade the people about the logic of his partisanship, he has founds new ground for new claims. An example of this is that the road to Bali was tarred because of his association with the ruling party. He and his collaborators have insisted that it was because of his prominence in national politics that his chiefdom was rewarded with the appointment of Bali subjects into positions of importance in the country. For instance, the former director of customs (and currently the CPDM mayor of Bali since 2007) and the minister of higher technical control were from Bali. Local gossip held that that the minister cited above had been appointed on Ganyonga's recommendation. Supporters of the chief also suggested that a government technical high school had been established in Bali in return for the fon's enduring commitment to the CPDM. In the next chapter I will show that Cameroon's democratic transition was only nominal thereby maintaining structures of patronage as exemplified by the above cases.

In general, the findings from this project confirm the logic of chiefs' decisions to participate in national politics on the side of the ruling party, despite its unpopularity among the masses (Nyamnjoh 2002). Nyamnjoh's contention is that most chiefs opted to join the ruling party due to growing uncertainty during the struggle for democracy in the early 1990s. Many chiefs reasoned that the best way of securing state protection and safeguarding their interests was to take sides with the CPDM because 'in the politics of give-and-take, it was out of the question not to expect to harvest where one had sown, and very dangerous to sow where one was not sure to harvest' (Nyamnjoh 2002:15). Essentially, this logic reveals that chiefs understood better than the masses that the so-called democratic transition was a mere farce.

In this light, certain chiefs have expressed their agency more than others. Some chiefs have also been more successful than others in negotiating their status and interests in the current democratic context. For instance, although fon Ganyonga failed in his bid to win the mayoral office in 1996, his counterpart in Balikumbat, fon Doh Gah Gwanyin succeeded to emerge (albeit by rigging and intimidation) as the only CPDM parliamentarian in a province dominated by the SDF. Despite their infighting, fons have made use of various associations such as NOWEFU to promote their individual and collective interests against other political competitors.

Conclusion

This chapter has explored the kinds of legitimacy claimed by fon Ganyonga in the democratic era; the extent to which such claims were accepted, contested or rejected by his subjects. Ganyonga's case is examined against the assumption that the introduction of democracy offered space to 'old political actors' to stage a comeback into the national political scene. The return of these actors was predicated on several claims for legitimacy but such claims by prominent chiefs were contested by the masses because they favoured the idea that chiefs should be neutral in partisan politics. Chiefs could win legitimacy on condition that they were non-partisan (or covertly partisan), and those who became involved with the CPDM especially in the higher ranks of the party were seen as betraying the will of the people by frustrating their attempts to vote the opposition into office.

Ganyonga's major challenge was to influence the course of local events in his chiefdom. One of the ways he tried to accomplish this was by standing as a candidate for the post of mayor in the council elections of January 1996. Although he failed to win the mayoral office, he did not give up his desire to win legitimacy and sought to pose as the protector of his people in other matters of chiefdom politics - such as lobbying for the promotion of his chiefdom to a fully fledged division, the campaign to restore a parliamentary constituency in Bali and his efforts in protecting the existing boundaries of the chiefdom against the claims of neighbouring chiefs. Although these issues seemed to have gained the support of the CPDM elite in the chiefdom, the masses have not been thrilled by them.

Despite his failures, many people interviewed for this study were delighted with Ganyonga's initial involvement in the lobby for the recognition of the Anglophone problem in the 1990s. Although he has not been consistent in public declarations concerning the Anglophone problem, he was lauded for having participated at significant events such as leading a delegation of North West fons to the historic All Anglophone Conference in 1993. He also accompanied elites of the North West in opposing the admission of Cameroon into the Commonwealth. In 2002 Ganyonga and several first class fons of the North West made an official trip to the presidency where they presented a memorandum in which they called for a solution to the Anglophone problem and the economic development of the province.

This notwithstanding, Ganyonga's relationship with his subjects has fluctuated between cordiality and antagonism. Subjects had mixed feelings about him not only because of his involvement in the CPDM but also because he was seen as not conducting himself properly as a 'father' should towards his children. At a particular period after 1996, subjects refused to provide free labour, a customary form of tribute to royalty. It was only after he allegedly placed a ban on 'death celebrations' that people were compelled to obey. Since then, observers have noted remarkable improvement in relations between Ganyonga and his subjects. Various accounts indicate that different quarters, groups and individuals now pay tribute to the fon usually in the form of firewood and, sometimes, palm wine. For example in 2002 the Christian community in Bali led by Fr. James Nsokika paid tribute to the fon in the form of food items and firewood. In return, the fon distributed salt to the subjects in line with the popular saying that no one enters the palace and comes out empty-handed. Growing disillusionment among the masses concerning the prospects for genuine democratic change has led some critics to limit their hostility towards the fon's political activities. The fact that people have thrown their weight behind the SCNC which champions the cause of Anglophone independence is an indication that people are fed up with the promises of political pluralism and the so-called democratic transition.

This chapter has analysed the changes that have occurred in Bali and accounted for the factors that brought about these changes particularly with respect to the relationship between the fon and his subjects. But an important question still remains unanswered: is the exhortation about the incompatibility of chiefs and democracy necessarily true of Bali? Although it appears so, a broader canvass is needed in order to paint the whole picture. My ethnographic findings reveal that chiefs can play a role in Cameroon's democracy on condition that they enter the political scene as 'neutral' mediators – a role favoured by the masses. The chief's predicament in the Cameroon grassfields should be understood in the context of the so-called democratic transition that took place in the 1990s. This case study shows that Ganyonga's claim to legitimacy in the democratic era was contested by the people not because 'chiefs' ought not to participate in the democratic process, but because he was seen to be siding with the state against them. The fact that Ganyonga failed to offer protection to his people, thereby leaving them at the mercy of state predation explains the people's initial hostility to the fon. The example of the SDO's visit to Bali in 2001 illustrates this claim. One can also recall the example of some chiefs in Ghana who were perceived by the people as willing tools of the government of the day (Boafo-Arthur 2001).

It is precisely because of chiefs' involvement in national politics on the side of the government that most chiefs have failed to assert themselves as alternative sites of power next to the state (cf. Geschiere 1993). Although by joining the CPDM many chiefs 'felt this was the best way of securing state protection and safeguarding their interests in a context of keen competition and differences along ethnic lines' (Nyamnjoh 2002:14-5), it is clear that most of their claims to legitimacy in this respect were undermined by the people. For instance, while the state continued to perceive these chiefs as vote-brokers in rural areas (Geschiere 1993; Oomen 2000), it is evident that chiefs have failed to live up to this expectation. As 'auxiliaries' of the administration, they were expected to play the role of gatekeepers through which the state could capture rural votes (cf. Jua 1995) but Ganyonga's case suggests that, far from being a vote-broker, he has actually become part and parcel of the state elite thereby failing to negotiate the desired rural votes on behalf of the state. Proof of this is the fact that the ruling party has not won a single election in Bali since 1996 despite relentless effort by the fon and the local CPDM elite.[101]

Ganyonga's loyalties do not lie with the state alone. While his subjects have contested his claim to certain kinds of legitimacy, they have in turn, accepted other claims. Ganyonga's predicament is therefore ambiguous. Some of his claims are accepted while others are not. Why are certain claims rejected and not others? Does this mean chiefs are more compatible with democracy in Tshivhase than in Bali? Do chiefs have the same meaning for people in Bali as in Tshivhase? These questions are essentially comparative and therefore deserve fresh focus. In the next chapter, I will compare and contrast the predicament of both chiefs and account for their similarities and differences. This approach will contribute to the reader's understanding of the democratic transition in both countries and indeed the nature of the postcolonial state in each case.

Chapter Six

Chieftaincy and democracy in comparative perspective

'Without systematic comparative studies anthropology will become only historiography and ethnography.' A. R. Radcliffe-Brown, Huxley Memorial Lecture, 1951

'Our first democratic elections were held in 1994. Some people are still waiting for the results.' [102]

In this final chapter I will focus on the comparative dimensions of the cases under study– that is, identifying and accounting for the differences and parallels that have been experienced by Tshivhase and Ganyonga with respect to social and political change in their various chiefdoms. A comparative study of this nature is a contribution to the 'frontier of recent anthropology' (Hannerz 1997:546) that involves 'multi-sited' studies (Marcus 1995). The objective here is to show the relevance of my findings to on-going discussions on chiefs and democratic transition in both countries. The next section discusses the relevance of these findings towards understanding the democratic transitions in South Africa and Cameroon and indeed, the nature of the South African and Cameroonian postcolonial states in the contemporary era.

Tshivhase and Bali Compared in the Democratic Era.

I will begin by showing the similarities between Chiefs Tshivhase and Ganyonga and those between the subjects of the two chiefdoms. To begin with, the positions and careers of both chiefs are quite similar. Both of them enjoy the prestige of coming from a line of powerful traditional rulers in their regions. Tshivhase for instance benefited from the prestige associated with his grandfather, Ratsimphi, who as described in chapter two was an icon of the liberation struggle in the 1940s until his death at the hands of the South African government. Ganyonga on the other hand, traces his descent to the legendary leader, Galega I, who was the first chief to accommodate the Germans in the hinterlands of the grassfields. Ganyonga's father also played a leading role in the struggle for the independence of the Southern Cameroons and was the architect of the House of Chiefs, later abolished in 1972. As a whole, both chiefs owe their current prominence partly to the legacy of their forebears.

The second similarity is that both chiefs occupy positions of prominence in national politics in their respective countries. Since 1994 Chief Tshivhase has occupied various portfolios in the ANC, first as a senator in Cape Town and from 1999 to 2005 as an ANC member in the Limpopo Provincial House of Assembly. He stepped down from this position in 2005 and chose to concentrate in running the Tshivhase Development Trust. Tshivhase's prominence in national politics tended to reinforce his popularity at the local level, making him the best-known Venda chief in post-apartheid South Africa. Fon Ganyonga on the other hand has also risen to national prominence following his co-optation into the Central Committee of the ruling CPDM party. In addition, he has participated in various aspects of provincial and national politics, such as the All Anglophone Conference which took place in Buea in 1993. Ganyonga also made national headlines when he decided to run for the office of mayor in his chiefdom.

Third, both chiefs have claimed legitimacy in the democratic era as chiefs and as modern politicians, thus arguing for the compatibility of chiefs and democracy. By combining his position as chief and ANC politician, Tshivhase has provided a shield for his people against the market-driven policies of the local council, which, as discussed in chapter three, are unfavourable to the rural poor. He benefited from the low esteem that his subjects have for the local council by introducing certain changes to customary practice, such as opening access to land to women and reducing the fee for allocating land to residents. Unlike other chiefs in the Venda area who did very little to stand up to the local council, Chief Tshivhase decided to back his subjects in refusing to pay for services they were not yet receiving. Ganyonga also made similar claims about his legitimacy as both chief and modern politician. Ganyonga argued his case on the basis of his ability to attract state-driven development to his chiefdom by lobbying for the chiefdom to be elevated to the level of a full-fledged administrative division. Among other claims, he also argued that he could serve as an entry point for locals to get into the administration – evidenced by the appointment of two Bali subjects into positions of prominence. Although some of his claims have been contested by the people (because they are based on elite interests), he nonetheless won credibility for his involvement in the Anglophone cause during the early 1990s, which until today, remains an extremely popular issue among his subjects and citizens of the North West Province. Thus, both chiefs have made different claims in similar contexts about the legitimacy of their participation in 'inventing' the future of their communities and countries. At issue is not whether specific claims were accepted or challenged by the masses, but that both chiefs have competed for and made strong claims for their own political space in the democratic era.

The fourth point is that both chiefs could be seen as agents vying for their own interests in contexts of keen competition. I will argue that both chiefs have been involved in safeguarding not only their own interests, but also those of other chiefs, through various lobby groups such as chiefs' organisations. In this connection, one should take into account the on-going contest among rival Venda chiefs discussed in chapter two. Chief Tshivhase has not only emphasised the autonomy of his chiefdom from other rival chiefdoms, but also sought to transform it into a powerful kingdom in which he could be recognised as king – without ostensibly, claiming jurisdiction over other Venda chiefdoms. Predictably, this may account for why he followed a process of appeasement with his headmen, instead of replacing them as anticipated by civic associations. He also made use of his personal dynamism by involving himself in the activities of youths in his chiefdom thereby winning their support and loyalty. In particular he was involved in promoting the *tshikona,* which he used as a rallying point for BaVenda resident in the cities. I am told that Chief Tshivhase took a *tshikona* troupe during his trips to Johannesburg, Cape Town and Durban to urge the BaVenda, regardless of their particular loyalties to rally behind him in order to promote their 'culture'. Many have interpreted this action as a hidden agenda to claim authority over all the BaVenda, a claim he has denied outright.

Fon Ganyonga also sought to safeguard his personal and political interests in a context of severe competition. The decision to become involved in the CPDM was in itself a calculated move by the fon to protect his interests against the uncertainties of the era. It has been argued already that the reintroduction of multiparty democracy in Cameroon offered new space for old political actors to re-enter the postcolonial political arena. However, at this juncture, chiefs had to compete not only with other government elites but also with the emerging opposition, some of who were their subjects. By choosing to participate in national politics on the side of the ruling party, Ganyonga was investing where he was sure to harvest. Although his determination to protect his interests was interpreted by the people as a betrayal against them, Ganyonga nonetheless tried to hedge his bets by patronising BANDECA activities.

I argued above that Chief Tshivhase and his colleagues in the Limpopo province also engaged in actions intended to protect and enhance the status of chiefs in the post-apartheid era. In this respect, I described the role played by the Congress of Traditional Leaders in South Africa (CONTRALESA) during the late 1980s. Although CONTRALESA was initially a regional formation, it soon became a national association after the ANC was unbanned in 1990. What I found particularly interesting about CONTRALESA was the way in which it appropriated the language of liberation by posing as a grassroots association together with civic movements and the United Democratic Front (UDF). Although CONTRALESA is dissatisfied with the current regime for downplaying the importance of traditional leaders, it has succeeded in securing some of the benefits it had bargained for during the CODESA talks of 1991-1993. It is principally due to CONTRALESA's pressure at the talks that there is a National House of Traditional Leaders and Provincial Houses in post-apartheid South Africa (even if the function of these houses is not clear even among the actors involved in running them).

Chiefs in the Bamenda grassfields also sought to foster their interests through various associations such as NOWEFCO and NOWEFU. In the past couple of years there has been substantial effort to unite the different associations into a single movement representing the collective interests of all chiefs and chiefdoms. In this respect considerable progress has been attained although relations between the NOWEFU leadership and fon Doh Gah Gwanyi remain acrimonious. Over the years, most fons of the North West Province have tended to speak with one voice on matters of common interests – such as awarding traditional titles to prominent government personalities. For example, in April 2001, the fons collectively granted the traditional title of "Pathfinder" to the then Prime Minister, Peter Musonge during his official visit to the province.

It is important to underscore the extent to which chiefs have successfully exercised agency both as individuals and groups by positioning themselves strategically as power-brokers between local, provincial and national governments. Most chiefs, especially those who enjoy membership in the CPDM and fons' associations have made strategic use of their membership to secure advantages for themselves and their chiefdoms, sometimes even against neighbouring chiefdoms. Through these associations, some chiefs have emerged as central actors in the drama of political transformation by penetrating the domain of elite circles, and indeed by becoming part and parcel of the ruling elite. Therefore, the point must be emphasised that chiefs do not serve the projects of tradition and the modern state only, but more important, that they also enter into transactions to secure and defend their personal interests.

The last similarity I wish to draw attention to is about the political situation of the subjects in the two chiefdoms. This point is not about the chiefs per se, but about the socio-political conditions experienced by the masses provoked by the introduction of democracy. My argument is that the introduction of democracy to both chiefdoms created contradictions that resulted in the renewed need for chiefs. In Tshivhase, this became manifest in the contradiction of introducing liberal democracy in neo-liberal circumstances (Comaroff and Comaroff 1999a, 2000). The point is that although South Africa's democratic transition was thoroughgoing, the history of dispossession and the present economic condition of the country exposed rural people to the chill winds of neo-liberalism. This contradiction therefore created the need for protection from these winds, which some chiefs were in a position to provide on condition that they had retained or earned enough legitimacy and prestige.

Cameroon's political transition was contradictory in that it introduced the form of democracy but not its substance, leaving the incumbent government in a position to prey on and manipulate the people and the opposition. This contradiction also created space for the re-entry of chiefs to serve as mediators and protectors of their people against the excesses of the government but on condition that such chiefs had retained enough credibility as well. Whether particular chiefs played this role or not is not an issue here. The parallel in both cases is that the contradictions experienced by the subjects created conditions for the re-emergence of chiefs.

Having examined the parallels between both chiefs and chiefdoms, I will proceed to explore and account for the difference in both cases. To this end, I will begin with the chiefs. The first major difference between Tshivhase and Ganyonga is in the way their political choices have affected their relationship with their subjects. In Tshivhase, the chief's involvement in national politics helped to reinforce his popularity at the base rather than undermine it. A majority of rural South Africans want the ANC to run the country because its reputation as liberator still outweighs the shortcomings of its local government system in rural areas. It was in this light that Tshivhase's popularity was enhanced relative to the Mphephu chiefs who were unable to switch camps to the ANC.[103] Tshivhase's involvement in national politics on the side of the ANC was therefore not in conflict with the popular choice of the people. Given his actions at the local level and his high-ranking status in the ANC, the people see Tshivhase as epitomising their hopes and aspirations.

By contrast, Ganyonga's involvement in national politics on the side of the CPDM helped to undermine his legitimacy in the eyes of his subjects. Unlike the ANC, which still enjoys the status of 'liberator', the CPDM in Cameroon is perceived by most people, particularly in the North West Province as the plague that must be avoided. The party and its officials are blamed for the social, economic and political problems of the country, and the SDF remains the most popular party in the North West Province. Although the SDF's fortunes have dwindled over the years, the CPDM still remains anathema in this region. By associating himself with the CPDM, Ganyonga was seen as sleeping with the enemy. One sees that although both chiefs rose to national prominence in the ruling parties in their respective countries, they differed considerably in terms of the credibility each built up with their subjects on account of this strategy.

The second contrast is the extent to which both chiefs could act as they liked. In other words, it is possible to contrast the degree of constraint on each chief to engage in specific actions – that is, the limit to their individual agencies. In this respect, I contend that although the two chiefs were agents and did make use of their ability to carry out different personal and political actions, it is evident from this study that Tshivhase had more scope for action than Ganyonga. Tshivhase could afford to introduce minor changes, with legal implications without necessarily running into trouble with the local council or the national government. In fact, he went as far as supporting his people in refusing to pay for services that were not yet delivered. He also stood up successfully to the Demarcation Board's attempt to take control of access to land in rural areas. Tshivhase's scope for action in many respects surpassed that of Ganyonga. The nature of the transition in Cameroon gave little option for chiefs including Ganyonga but to toe the line or see their status undermined by the state or their remuneration suspended. Many chiefs for instance had very little option but to throw in their lot with the CPDM. But even with this constraint, Ganyonga could still participate in certain activities such as the Anglophone conference, which was interpreted by the national government as subversive. My argument therefore does not suggest that Ganyonga could not act as he wished, but that the scope for such action was limited when compared to that of Chief Tshivhase. This contrast will be discussed further in the section on democratic transition in both countries.

While both chiefs share several similarities and differ on two significant bases, analysis also point to two main differences between the subjects of both chiefdoms. Subjects in both chiefdoms differed significantly in terms of the issues that were of local concern to them. In Tshivhase, the main problem was about subsistence and economic viability while in Bali the question was about the fon's failure to provide his subjects with the desired political protection. In other words, people in Tshivhase were preoccupied with economic issues while those in Bali were particularly concerned about political matters. To put this into perspective, it should be emphasised that people in Tshivhase were concerned about issues such as employment, better housing, food, water and electricity. I have already provided explanation for the high levels of unemployment in Tshivhase brought about by factors such as the closure or relocation of nearby industries and the reduced level of labour migration from the region. A few informants also blamed the high levels of unemployment on the expulsion of workers by commercial farmers. These factors accounted for the widespread protest against the TLC's attempt to market its services among the rural poor. There was deep disillusionment among the rural population owing to the great expectations many had about the supposed benefits of freedom and democracy. The reality however, is that the local council is not in a position to create jobs and given the economic circumstances in the country, the government is in little position to do the same. This has been left in the hands of the private sector and Venda seems to be at a disadvantage in attracting such 'developers'. This accounts partly for Chief Tshivhase's promotion of the Tshivhase Development Trust as a private initiative intended to alleviate the lot of the rural poor.

In Bali on the other hand, people were irked by the fon's reluctance to provide them with the desired protection from state predation. Although residents wanted economic development (which the chief claimed he could deliver via his association with the state), they did not want this at the expense of their newly gained freedom. But, as it became obvious, the freedoms were only nominal, not real. The people did not want the state to manage their resources such as water supply (the reason why they burnt down the SNEC office) but to maintain control over their resources under the auspices of the fon.

Several factors might account for the above difference although one specific issue stands out. I argue that this difference can be explained in terms of the different levels of economic development that each of the societies has undergone. In Tshivhase the long-term transformation has been from a peasant economy to one based on wage (industrial) labour. This means that the proportion of people relying on subsistence farming today is very small. In Bali, on the other hand, the economy is based on a combination of subsistence agriculture and wage labour. Indeed, the proportion of the population relying on subsistence agriculture is huge and even those employed in the wage economy tend to supplement their income with subsistence farming. Furthermore, although both societies are rural, they can be contrasted by their land tenure systems. While the chief in Tshivhase plays an extremely important role in the allocation and control of land, in Bali the chief's role in this respect is largely limited to ritual. It means that effective control of the land is vested in the subjects rather than the fon. In Tshivhase, by contrast, the chief or headman places restrictions on how a subject may put his or her land to use. More often than not, the land allocated to people is so small that even if they desired to engage in gardening, this would be practically impossible. But in Bali, most subjects own land and practice farming as a basic means of survival, even though they experience high levels of unemployment. Thus the different levels of economic development and socio-economic organisation accounts for a key difference between the plight of the subjects in Tshivhase and Bali.

The next point of difference is that chieftaincy has different meanings for the people in Tshivhase and Bali. Borrowing from Benedict Anderson (1991), West and Kloeck-Jensen (1999:484) contend that 'all authority, along with the community over which it is exercised, is "imagined", meaning invented, created, produced and reproduced in the midst of an ever-changing historical context.' They argue further that chieftaincy does not only have different levels of authority, but also different kinds of meaning for the people over whom this authority is exercised (cf. West and Kloeck-Jensen 1999:484). Failure to see these distinctions, they argue, not only muddles the historical debate on 'traditional authority' but also contributes to the 'danger of implementing political reforms that produce a "tradition" both unrecognisable and highly destructive to the lives of the local communities.'

Chieftaincy has meaning to the people in Tshivhase insofar as the chief can play the role of protector of the poor, at least in the short run. Although Venda has a long history of chieftaincy and powerful chiefs, the normative distinction between the office and the person became blurred during the apartheid period, especially in the 1980s when civic movements penetrated the political landscape in rural areas. It was during this period that the civic under the auspices of the United Democratic Front called for the abolition of chieftaincy in order to make room for peoples' power. Although calls for the abolition of chieftaincy were premature, as evidenced by the new role of chiefs in Tshivhase, it is a crucial aspect of difference between chieftaincy in Tshivhase and Bali. Many of the informants I interviewed hardly made reference to chieftaincy as the guardian of their culture or 'tradition' although a few maintained that chiefs represented their past. Ironically, their lives were affected on a daily basis by the authority of the chief and headmen. It was to the chief's kraal that they took their disputes, registered customary marriages, applied for land and so on. Their lives were not detached in any small way from the institution of chieftaincy. But as indicated above, most people conceptualised the role of chiefs from a functional perspective. Chieftaincy represented no intrinsic values, nor was there any deep sense of attachment to the institution. For instance, people no longer paid tribute (such as material gifts) to the chiefs although they used to do so during the apartheid period, of course under compulsion. Some informants observed that if the local council were popular and worked in favour of the rural poor, they would prefer it to the chiefs because while they could vote the councillors into office, they could not do the same with chiefs.

In Bali, on the contrary, chieftaincy had a deeper significance to the subjects than observed in Tshivhase. Although chiefs did not exercise the same intrusive authority over subjects in Bali as in Tshivhase, people felt that chiefs played a role far more significant to them than the state. This particular point was also advanced as a reason why they loathed the idea of their chief taking sides with the government. People also made reference to chieftaincy as a sacred institution, embodying their religious beliefs and customs. For instance, there could be no 'death-celebration' without prior sanction from the palace. The chief also received tribute (firewood and palm wine) from the subjects and was expected to perform his sacred role in ensuring the fertility of the land, of cleansing the chiefdom and transmitting the blessings of the ancestors. The chief in the Bamenda grassfields, to borrow from Jean-Pierre Warnier (1993) is perceived as a 'container holding a number of ancestral substances' which he redistributes among his subjects for the well-being of the commonwealth. Thus the institution of chief in Bali had deeper ritual implications than in Tshivhase. Chieftaincy, to the people was not only a socio-political organisation but also a sacred institution. Although the chief was blamed for poor conduct, the office of chief was seen as distinct from the office-bearer. Lastly, a survey of the history did not reveal that there had been at any stage, a clamour for the abolition of the institution. Perhaps, this particular observation would be different if the people had other credible alternatives. And this does not imply that things will always be the same given the possibility that an established order of this nature can be questioned. But as Bourdieu (1977) points out, it takes more than just a crisis to produce critical discourse about an institution of this nature, which appears 'self-evident' to the people. The main variation between the people in Tshivhase and their counterparts in Bali is that they hold different meanings for chieftaincy. In other words, the idea of chieftaincy is 'imagined' differently by the subjects in both chiefdoms and these imaginings have been subjected to changing historical contexts. Building on this distinction, there is need to revisit Barbara Oomen's notion of 'retraditionalisation', mentioned earlier in chapter one.

Oomen (2000) makes use of the concept of 'retraditionalisation' to explain the unexpected popularity and renewed loyalty towards the chiefs she observed in the field. In her study of social change in the Mamone chiefdom in the Limpopo Province, Oomen observed that what was going on at the time of her research could be described as retraditionalisation. By this concept, she meant the renewed sense of respect for chieftaincy and the popularity of the chief among the people. Based on a survey, she concluded that up to 73% of her respondents had accepted that they were loyal to their chief. She contrasted this 'renewed' importance of chiefs to the apartheid era when the comrades and the UDF advocated the abolition of chieftaincy. Although she does not conceptualise tradition as a fixed category, her use of the concept – retraditionalisation, suggests the view that Africans are obsessed with *tradition* regardless of how much 'modernity' they have acquired. Possibly, retraditionalisation implies that Africans can be equated with 'tradition' and will invariably return to their so-called 'roots' irrespective of their modern status or achievements. Patrick Chabal argues that Africanists need to exercise caution in their choice of words to 'explain' Africa. He suggests that Africanists should 'search for the concepts and the vocabulary which will make it possible to advance insight into the realities of contemporary Africa' (Chabal 1996:50). This view is echoed by another scholar who contends that 'being African is neither exclusively a matter of tradition and culture, nor exclusively a matter of modernity and citizenship' because 'Africans are simultaneously modernising their traditions and traditionalising their modernities' (Nyamnjoh 2002a). Concepts such as retraditionalisation therefore, tend to blur rather than illuminate one's understanding of the issues at stake.

A survey of the classical literature reveals that chiefs have been popular at particular instances and unpopular at other times. In describing the increased respect and popularity of chiefs as retraditionalisation, complex processes going on in the chiefdom are reduced to the simple equation of tradition. To buttress my argument, let me extend my discussion about the different ways in which chieftaincy was imagined in Bali and Tshivhase. Chief Tshivhase for example, accepted that although he was a champion of 'cultural revival' in Venda, his popularity was not based exclusively on this. As a matter of fact the people's esteem for him was based on his innovative land policy and the promises he made concerning the development of his chiefdom. This point re-emphasises the economic predicament of the subjects rather than their so-called yearning for their roots. The developments in Mamone were not unique or unprecedented. Parallels have been recorded and analysed even as far back as the 1940s.

In his 'Analysis of a Social Situation in Modern Zululand', Max Gluckman demonstrated that the Zulu king and his *indunas* enjoyed renewed loyalty on account of the fact that much of their powers had been curtailed. Although this situation was ironical, it was apparent that the chiefs had 'little political influence in … fundamental economic aspects of Zululand life' (ibid. 18). Gluckman argued further that 'though the Regent was not officially recognised as head of the Zulu nation by Government, all Zulu regarded him as supreme over them' (ibid. 24). It was in this respect that 'tension against Government' was expressed through the Regent. What is obvious here is that at this particular era, the Zulu regent became quite popular among his subjects for serving as a means through which dissatisfaction about the colonial government could be channelled. In this connection, it is likely that the people would have questioned his authority if they saw him as siding too closely with the colonial state. The people's renewed respect for the regent was not necessarily out of respect for tradition, or because they had retraced their path in the dark forest of modernity, but because they stood to benefit by showing deference to the traditional leader.

A parallel can be drawn from the above example regarding the contemporary situation in Tshivhase. Similar to the Zulu Regent in the 1940s, Chief Kennedy Tshivhase has also become a channel through which subjects' dissatisfaction with local government is expressed. Although Chief Tshivhase also represents the government of the day, his subjects see this as a credit rather than an issue for contention. It means that Chief Tshivhase's role is like a double-edged sword, which cuts in both directions. He legitimises the central government in his chiefdom while simultaneously exploiting the shortcomings of the local council to his own advantage. His popularity is due to several factors, the least of them being his role in the revival of Venda culture.

Implications for Democratic Transition and the State

Having examined the parallels and differences between the chiefs and chiefdoms, I will devote this section to an in-depth analysis of the democratic transitions in both countries. The main objective here is to establish and analyse what the findings above tell us of the democratic transitions in South Africa and Cameroon, and indeed about the South African and Cameroon postcolonial states. Analysis in this section is inspired by a major distinction already discussed above. I noted that one of the key differences between Chief Tshivhase and fon Ganyonga was the fact that the former had more scope for agency than the latter.

South Africa's democratic transition represents one of the most fundamental political transformations in the late 20th century. This consisted of a radical shift from an apartheid/authoritarian state to a modern democratic state, built on the principles of equality and racial harmony. Besides having one of the most 'progressive' constitutions in Africa, South Africa possesses 'all the institutions and mechanisms which are normally understood to constitute a fully fledged liberal democracy'[104] (Lodge 1999:68).

While these institutions and mechanisms are necessary, however, they are not sufficient to make democracy work, though they can influence its consolidation significantly. This notwithstanding, some scholars are worried about the workability of the new democratic system 'in which representative politics is overwhelmed by one large party and in which the prospects of any alternation of parties in government are pretty remote' (Lodge 1999:68). Given the historical legacy of racial conflict and oppression in South Africa, it is feared that the black majority will remain 'fairly uncritical, or undemanding' of the ANC, thus leaving 'its leadership scope for plenty of misbehaviour.' (Lodge 1999:68). If such is the case, then this threat is more imminent in the Limpopo Province than anywhere else in South Africa, given the extreme popularity of the ANC in the province. Indeed Maloka (1996:85) has pointed out that in Limpopo Province the ANC is the 'only game in town'.

However, if democratisation has brought new hope and benefits to the metropolitan urbanites of South Africa, it has on the other hand, provoked new anxieties and betrayed the hopes of many rural and 'township' citizens such as those in Tshivhase. In this regard, I have already explored the contradictions of 'liberation' under a neo-liberal economic context (cf. Comaroff and Comaroff 1999, 2000) and how citizens have reacted and adapted to these new demands.

Nonetheless, an important question that needs to be considered in the light of developments in South Africa is: does the discourse of democratisation as propounded

[95]

in the African context, provide the most appropriate framework for inventing the future, given the pluralistic composition of African societies? (Fisiy 1995: 49). Of course, the answer is negative. Democratisation in South Africa has had the latent function of producing new exclusions as seen earlier in this chapter. Such exclusions are not only in terms of the limits to which citizens can exercise their economic rights, but also political – because a significant proportion of 'old political actors' (chiefs) feel sidelined by the politics of the new dispensation. So, what do these findings tell us about the nature of the South African postcolonial state?

A crucial point is that although the postcolonial state in South Africa has deracialised, it is yet to consolidate its democratic achievements (Deegan 1999:156). The state seems to be caught between a rock and a hard place. It is simultaneously obsessed with the discourse of modernisation and nation-building while espousing the virtue of African renaissance and 'ubuntu', although it is unclear what these concepts represent. Nevertheless, there is a growing perception especially among the new black elite that tradition and chieftaincy are obstacles to the modern projects of the postcolonial state, granting that chieftaincy tends to promote 'tribal' consciousness (Maloka 1996:193).

While chiefs insist that the government does not seem to know 'what to do with the indigenous systems'[105] the government proposes that chiefs shall 'complement the role of government in rural areas' (Department of Provincial and Local Government 2002:21) in its effort to 'democratise' development.[106] But thus far, national government's discourse about development is yet to become a reality in most rural areas. This does not imply however, that urban areas have benefited more from the new political dispensation than their rural counterparts. In fact, one needs to emphasise the legacy of the apartheid state on contemporary socio-economic conditions. And the most vicious of these legacies is the sustained poverty in both rural and urban areas. Indeed, some analysts are of the opinion that the post-apartheid state is characterised by 'a radically widening chasm between rich and poor' (Comaroff and Comaroff 1999b:19) and this can be illustrated by the new black elite's engagement in the conspicuous consumption of prized commodities while the bulk of ordinary South Africans are still trapped in shacks, shantytowns, joblessness, and uncertainty (Nyamnjoh 2000:13). Furthermore, it is apparent that the government has failed in redistributing land as a mode of poverty alleviation.[107] In 1994 the government promised to redistribute 30% of white-owned land within five years but today, only 2% of the 87% of the best land in the country owned by whites has been redistributed (Commey 2002:12-16). The fact that democratisation has not necessarily transformed the economic conditions of the bulk of ordinary South Africans raises more questions than it answers. Thus a 'new' kind of apartheid (economic in nature) has come into force although not sanctioned by law. This kind of apartheid still thrives in many respects and poses the greatest threat to South Africa's new democracy (cf. Ake 2000; Commey 2002).

In many rural areas of South Africa including Tshivhase, chiefs still perform judicial functions based on apartheid legislation. During the apartheid era, chiefs were not allowed to try criminal cases such as murder, abortion, witchcraft, rape and bribery among others, a list of which could be found in the Government Gazette.[108] But today, some chiefs are dealing with criminal cases[109] owing to the 'overburdened' nature of magistrates' courts and the complex procedures that citizens are expected to undergo in order to seek justice. This is an area that needs further investigation. However this ambiguity is reflected not only in the functions performed by chiefs, but also among the people who prefer that a strict distinction should be maintained between tribal areas and urban territories. This trend is directly in response to the subjects' realisation that the capacity to exercise one's citizenship is inevitably tied to a price, which can be achieved only by those who can afford. This has given rise to a situation where people have appropriated not only both statuses of citizen and subject (Nyamnjoh 2002b) but also tend to juggle between these categories depending on the circumstances. Thus, the contradictions resulting from the political transition in South Africa permitted some traditional authorities to make new claims for legitimacy. This has given rise to a postcolonial state that is a hybrid in many respects - although its official discourse is that of a 'modern' and 'progressive' state (South African Constitution 1996:21).

The democratic transition in Cameroon, unlike in South Africa, consisted of a minimal shift from authoritarian or monolithic rule to multiparty democracy leaving the incumbent government in power. Some scholars have described this particular transition not only as a 'passive revolution'[110] but also as democratisation from 'above' or rather, a conservative adaptation to demands for revolutionary reform (Sindjoun 1999:1-5). It seems to me that fon Ganyonga and his colleagues in the North West Province, grasped this particular aspect of Cameroon's transition more than their subjects and other political actors. This was apparent when they opted to participate in party politics on the side of the ruling party, granting that they could not risk to sow where they were not sure to reap. Such manoeuvring, according to Nyamnjoh confirms the claim that 'political choices are predicated upon vested interests which are not fixed and which along with these choices are subject to re-negotiation with changing circumstances' (Nyamnjoh 2002:11).

Be that as it may, a major contrast between the democratic transitions in South Africa and Cameroon as seen through the predicament of chiefs is that, Chief Tshivhase had more choice and freedom in terms of his political actions than his counterpart in Bali. It means that it was in Ganyonga's interest to be active in the politics of the CPDM rather than in any other party. This view can be buttressed by the fact that not all chiefs in the grassfields have been successful in negotiating their positions in relation to the state. From the vantage point of the postcolonial state, 'a chief who is not the compliant servant of government represents the resistance of local community and its ruling group to the intervention of central government in local affairs' (von Trotha, 1996:83) even when this is not necessarily the case. Several chiefs are known to have been at the mercy of the state especially those without CPDM connections such as the fon of Fungom who ran into trouble many times with civil administrators in his chiefdom owing to his SDF-inclination. This underscores the claim that in Cameroon 'the most unpardonable crime is that of disloyalty to the president' and 'political allegiance to the CPDM remains one of the surest guarantees against' government persecution (Nyamnjoh, 1999:106-7).[111]

There is some consensus among scholars that Cameroon's democratic transition has not only stalled (Bayart, Ellis, and Hibou 1999; Nyamnjoh 1999, 2002a; Ake 2000; Mbaku 2002) but also that the state in Cameroon seems to be reverting to the authoritarian era (Bratton and Van de Valle 1997:235). [112] The state is still seen as predatory, patrimonial, and symmetrical with the ruling CPDM. In a commentary on Cameroon, Nyamnjoh (2002a) contends that to most Cameroonians, democracy is perceived as a cosmetic device 'used to justify excesses of various kinds, especially by those determined to celebrate the status quo.' In another context, he describes Cameroon's democratic transition as pseudo and as recycled monolithism. This pseudo transition gave rise to a 'T-shirt-slogan' democracy where the power elite set the agenda for the people, 'use them to serve their ends and at the end of the day, abandon them to the misery and ignorance to which they are accustomed' (Nyamnjoh 1999:115). Liberalisation in Cameroon has thus not led to the consolidation of democracy.

This is not to insinuate that Cameroon is incapable of sustaining a liberal and democratic society given the extensive socio-political networks 'from below' that advocate democratic change on a daily basis. Unfortunately, the crises affecting many opposition parties, especially the SDF[113] begins to cast doubts as to how long the bulk of Cameroonians may have to wait before enjoying the fruits of their struggle. In fact, many recent commentators have observed that there is growing apathy among citizens in Cameroon, which can be contrasted to the early 1990s when there was overwhelming enthusiasm for democratic change (cf. Mbaku 2002).

To illustrate this growing disillusionment, let us take a cursory look at the performance of the SDF and other political parties since 1997. In October 1997 the SDF boycotted the presidential election for reasons that have been explored before - due partly to the lack of an independent electoral body. The incumbent, Paul Biya consequently won about 92% of the votes, reminiscent of the one-party era. Although the SDF boycotted the presidential election, it had participated in the parliamentary election that took place earlier in May 1997 and had won 26% of the 180 seats in parliament. Following the recent legislative and council elections in that took place on 30 June 2002, the SDF's dwindling fortunes became apparent when it won only 22 seats (with 20 from the North West Province) representing only 12% of the total seats in parliament. On the contrary, the CPDM increased its hold in the house by winning 149 of the 180 seats, representing a landslide victory of about 82%.[114] Although the opposition and other independent observers complained about massive rigging and the oppressive tactics by government administrators to secure a CPDM victory, not much could be done to reverse or amend such irregularities.[115]In July 2007, the number of SDF seats in parliament reduced from 22 to only 14, again underscoring the resilience of the CPDM and the improbability of Cameroonians changing their government through the ballot – particularly if the same institutions or mutations of these continue to organise elections as they've done in the past.

What do the findings above tell us about the postcolonial state in Cameroon? The answer to this question lies in the experiences of grassfields chiefs in general and fon Ganyonga of Bali in particular. According to Achille Mbembe, 'the postcolony is a particularly revealing (and rather dramatic) stage on which are played out the wider problems of subjection and its corollary, discipline' (Mbembe 1992:555). This is 'intermediated' by co-optation. The state in Cameroon continues to thrive on patron-client networks as a defining mechanism for entry and survival in the postcolony. In a patronage system like Cameroon's, clients are not expected to challenge their masters. Civil servants, bureaucratic elites and chiefs (as auxiliaries of the administration) are all expected to perform their role in order to perpetuate the status quo. Taking the example of chiefs in the grassfields, one sees that most of them are not simply CPDM members out of choice as they would want us to believe, but mainly as a result of the complex dynamics that surround clientelistic politics. The fon of Bali for instance repeatedly argued that it was only by actively supporting the CPDM that he could ensure the territorial integrity of his chiefdom against rival neighbours. He was also behind a lobby that advocated the elevation of his chiefdom to a fully-fledged administrative division based on his support for the CDPM. But to a large extent, Ganyonga was particularly keen on protecting his own interests in a context of acute competition. Mbembe sees this sort of relationship as an 'illicit cohabitation', contrary to mainstream classification which tends to emphasise the bipolarity between resistance and collaboration. He argues further that such illicit cohabitation is fraught with familiarity and domesticity whose principal motif is to maintain and propagate the interests of the different political actors implicated in this relationship.

The domesticity of the relationship between chiefs and bureaucratic elites could be seen in the ways that chiefs invented neo-traditional titles to co-opt the latter, which, in turn, granted them access to the corridors of state power. In April 2001 for example, the fons of the North West Province collectively awarded the title of 'Pathfinder' to the then Prime Minister, Peter Musonge during his official visit to the province. One could also recall the award of a prestigious title in 2001 by the fon of Nso to a government minister, Dr Peter Abety. These kinds of exchange and domesticity constitute what Mbembe refers to as the postcolonial subject's ability to bargain in a conceptual market place.

Although there is much bargaining in the background, many of the political actions of postcolonial subjects could also be understood from the perspective of 'performance'[116]. The predatory state continues to perceive chiefs as vote-brokers and expects them to play this role. Little wonder that chiefs in the grasslands were implicated in the rigging of past elections, as will be seen shortly. As clients of the system, chiefs consistently endeavoured to perform the 'rituals' of facilitating CPDM victory in their respective chiefdoms, more often than not without success. It is reported that during the parliamentary elections of May 1997 a chief, seeing that the defeat of the CPDM was inevitable, escaped with the ballot box into the inner quarters of his palace where commoners had no access. The Commonwealth Report of 1997 condemned such practices in their report as follows:

> While acknowledging the important role of traditional chiefs and quarter heads in the social context of Cameroon, we consider the location of polling stations inside or near private residence as being prejudicial to progress that was done in a bid to establish a neutral and transparent electoral system[117].

Incidents have been reported of chiefs trying to play the role of 'decentralised despots' ironically in the democratic era. In Tabenken, a small chiefdom in the Donga-Mantung Division, the fon expressed his disappointment over the defeat of the CPDM by ordering the arrest of an SDF councillor in his chiefdom. It is reported that the SDF official, Florence Njobe, had refused a bribe of 20 000 CFA Francs from the fon intended to convince her to facilitate a CPDM victory. Florence Njobe had refused to collaborate on the grounds that her party did not approve of corruption. She claimed that she 'reminded the fon that he too had been in the SDF party and that as SDF councillors, we vowed never to receive bribe.'[118] One can see from the preceding accounts that although chiefs bargain in the 'conceptual market place' of the postcolonial state, they are also performers. In this regard, one cannot afford to forget the postcolonial chief's talent for play and his sense of fun, which makes him '*homo ludens par excellence*' (Mbembe 1992:557), that is, when one considers absurd incidents such as running away with a ballot box into secret chambers or arresting a subject for refusing to accept a bribe. Be that as it may, one sees from the above and previous accounts, that failure to perform the rituals 'that ratify the *commandement's* own institutionalisation' results in a situation of violence.

If one takes into account the view that Cameroon's democratic transition is located between 'survival' and the potential reversal to authoritarianism, it follows that the postcolonial state in Cameroon is trapped within a liminal experience that seems to have no end. This liminality, ironically, suggests more of continuity than what one might normally consider a *rite de passage*. To substantiate this point, I propose to examine three dominant features that continue to give shape to the postcolonial state in Cameroon.

Many scholars have described Cameroon as a classic patrimonial state. This involves a 'highly personal and clientelistic type of rule involving massive redistribution of state resources' (Gabriel 1999:173). Such a system breeds stability and instability simultaneously. This means that elites make heavy use of state resources to meet clientelistic needs, which tends to undermine the very stability it purports to foster. Under Ahidjo, patrimonial rule was coterminous with presidentialism, which meant the total concentration of power in one person and one institution – 'la présidence' (Prouzet 1974:151-86 cited in Gabriel 1999:175). Ahidjo saw himself as the father of the nation and the supreme guide who had the exclusive right to conduct the postcolony towards development. To achieve his goal, he built a large clientelistic network reaching practically every corner of the country, which meant that the emerging elite owed everything to him – (jobs, licences, contracts, projects) and were expected to show gratitude accordingly (Gabriel 1999). Under Biya, patrimonial rule continued more or less in the same manner despite his claim that he introduced liberal democracy in Cameroon through his New Deal government. But since his coming to power in 1982, Biya has epitomised the postcolony in various forms: he is the fon of fons, the 'indomitable lion of Cameroon' and the number one sportsman in the country. Biya is thanked for every ministerial or high office appointment, which is usually seen as an act of benevolence. Once appointed, ministers usually go to their home villages to gather support and give gratitude to the Head of State who is said to have rewarded their allegiance to the CPDM by appointing 'a son or daughter of the soil' as the case may be.

Furthermore, in Cameroon as in many other African countries, power is closely associated with 'the capacity to consume, or the ability 'to eat', as expressed both literally and figuratively in many indigenous languages' (Schatzberg 1993:445). There is an interesting link here between 'redistribution' as seen above and consumption. This, I suppose introduces what Bayart refers to as 'politics of the belly' which incidentally is a concept borrowed from Cameroon. In Cameroon, frequent reference is made to the 'national cake' as a source for political competition. Every appointment to high office is followed by an emphasis 'on the benefits of the position to the individual concerned, but hardly ever with the responsibilities that go with the office' (Nyamnjoh 1999:106). This has been captured by Bayart (1989) when he refers to appointments and disappointments as 'On lui a donné la bouffe' or 'On lui a enlevé la bouffe' ('They have been given something to eat, or They have had the right to eat taken away' (Schatzberg, 1993:447). Even after Cameroon's so called 'passive revolution' not much has changed. While Bayart's description befits the authoritarian era quite rightly, Nyamnjoh's assessment of the situation addresses the post-1990 era. According to him, 'the struggles in the name of democracy seem more like the war of the bellies where the 'eaters' ('les bouffeurs') are questioned, but seldom the act of 'eating' ('bouffer'). Patrons and clients may be questioned, but not patronage or patrimonialism. To many people in or seeking high office, Cameroon is little more than a farm tended by God but harvested by man.' Clearly, the politics of the belly has exacerbated in the democratic era. The 'war of bellies' has become so endemic that even opposition parties that wish to replace the ruling party have failed to rise above such practices. Instead they could be seen, as seeking to replace the ruling bellies rather than the welfare of those they claim to represent (Nyamnjoh 1999:114).

From the discussions above, one sees that the democratic transitions in South Africa and Cameroon represent two contrasting trajectories. South Africa's transition can be described as thoroughgoing while Cameroon's can be seen as cosmetic. As argued above, the degree of democratic reform introduced by each of the countries can be discerned partly in the degree of choice and freedom exercised by the chiefs. My argument therefore, is that Ganyonga had fewer options to manoeuvre than his counterpart in Tshivhase because Cameroon's political transition introduced only the form of democracy without its content.

Conclusion

We must ground our political analysis of contemporary events in the deep history of Africa, that is, the history which connects the present with the colonial and precolonial past'[119]

Does it follow from the preceding argument that chieftaincy and democracy are compatible in South Africa and not in Cameroon? Having examined the nature of the political transitions in both countries, it would be unfair to equate South Africa's democratic status with Cameroon's. Therefore, an answer to the above question should take into account the fact that both cases are not only complex, but do not also represent the experiences of chiefs in other regions of both countries. I have argued throughout this book that the contradictory nature of the political transitions in both countries created conditions for the entry of 'old political actors'. Not all of these old political actors gained credibility with the people or even with the state, thus the extent to which each of the chiefs succeeded depended on other intervening variables. These variables did not in themselves make chieftaincy compatible with democracy, because in principle, liberal democracy has no space for hereditary leadership. But because the praxis of liberal democracy was not limited to the political sphere, it meant that there was room for other actors who derived their authority not on democratic bases. Such was the supposed 'compatibility' between chiefs and democracy in Tshivhase, but not necessarily in South Africa as a whole. On the other hand, although Cameroon's cosmetic transition provided room for the entry of old political actors, they could do so on condition that they threw in their lot with the CPDM government, rather than with the emerging opposition or with the people whom they claimed to represent. Thus chiefs did not argue their case on the basis of compatibility with democracy, but on *survival* in a context of uncertainty and keen competition with other actors, especially the new ones who commanded great following among the people.

This ethnography makes a case for the importance of comparative research on chiefs in the era of democracy and the predicaments they face therein. I argue that contrary to exhortations about the incompatibility of chiefs and democracy, the reality is that political transition in both countries produced contradictions which created space for chiefs to fill, but on condition that they were able to draw on different kinds of legitimacy and had not been discredited by their past or existing involvement with the postcolonial state.

Although both chiefs appeared very similar in terms of their political careers, they differed along several lines. This was evident in the fact that whereas Chief Tshivhase gained popularity owing to his involvement in national politics in the ANC, Ganyonga became quite unpopular among his subjects during the same period. However, the fact that both chiefs have stayed on in national politics for over a decade and have succeeded in various ways to legitimise their positions as chief, interrogates exhortations about the inevitable demise of chieftaincy and its incompatibility with democracy.

Mainstream scholarship recognises that contemporary chiefs are located between the sphere of custom and the modern projects of the postcolonial state (cf. Geschiere 1993). In this sense, they are both traditional and modern simultaneously or rather, they are neither completely modern nor completely traditional but a product of both influences (Nyamnjoh 2002). In Ghana for example, the state recognises the fact that 'chieftaincy constitutes a major resource that could be officially tapped in reinforcing the modern government structure' (Boafo-Arthur 2001:8). Similarly, the South African Constitution recognises the fundamental role of chiefs in the domain of custom and tradition.[120] In Tshivhase as in Bali, the chief represents 'tradition' and the modern state. By transcending the divide between the realm of traditional leadership and that of modern politics, Chief Tshivhase has emerged as a chief placed at the intersection between the state and the traditional community. The same applies to fon Ganyonga who is also a modern politician and a traditional leader simultaneously.

I agree with other scholars that chiefs today are intercalary figures but this by itself is nothing new. It should be emphasised that many of the discussions tend to treat the intercalary status of contemporary chiefs as a new phenomenon whereas this is not the case. This reminds one on the need to ground one's analysis in the 'deep history of Africa' as suggested by Chabal (1996:51). In chapter one, I talked of the need to make use of the classical anthropological literature on chiefs especially those written by Gluckman (1940) and Schapera (1970). I have found these works useful for a general understanding of the intercalary status of chiefs since colonial times. In his study of chiefs and social change among the Tswana, Schapera for example observed that in the course of time, the chiefs became 'relatively less important as agents of social change' and by the 1940s many of them had been reduced to the status of subordinate government officers (ibid. 238). This notwithstanding, they still maintained a dominant role in the control of customary issues. Similarly, Gluckman (1940) observed in his article: 'Chief and Native Commissioner in Modern Zululand' that although the chief had become inextricably tied to the colonial government, he nevertheless, continued to play an important role in customary affairs. 'Not only does he lead them [subjects] in their opposition to Government, but he also has for them a value the magistrate cannot have' (Gluckman 1963:173). In fact, this intercalary position seems to have been cemented in the postcolonial era. Today, chiefs tend to mediate local realities and larger spheres of national importance in addition to their role as 'guardians of tradition' irrespective of how elusive such tradition is. Some chiefs also serve as negotiators for their subjects 'to enter the realm of public affairs, … especially … the neo-patrimonial, clientelist network' (von Trotha, 1996:88).[121]

In addition to serving a double project, chiefs also serve a third category - themselves. In other words, chiefs are calculating agents, whose actions and aspirations seek to perpetrate their personal interests. Besides serving the projects of the modern state, chiefs desire to extend their personal influence, secure more advantages for themselves and consolidate their hegemonic grip over their communities. Chiefs engage constantly in different fields of action with their subjects and the state, which could be interpreted variously as performance, adaptation and improvisation. This ethnography is replete with illustrations of the various ways in which chiefs expressed their agentive endowments. It is evident from the case studies that the chiefs and their subjects are undergoing various kinds of transformation – political, economic and cultural, and have appropriated different mechanisms to meet these new challenges. Chiefs in particular have had to make decisions that affect not only their own individual interests, but also those of their subjects.

The experiences of both chiefs however, provide a window through which we can appreciate the course of social and political transformation in their respective countries. Seen through the eyes of their people, both chiefs still have the potential to play a key role in the contradictions resulting from political change. On the whole, it is apparent that chiefs, and the institutions they represent, are not relics of a glorious past, but rather, are 'defined, animated, and in some cases produced by the contemporary politics of the modern nation-state' (Lindstrom and White 1997:13).

Appendix One

Genealogy of Tshivhase Chiefs

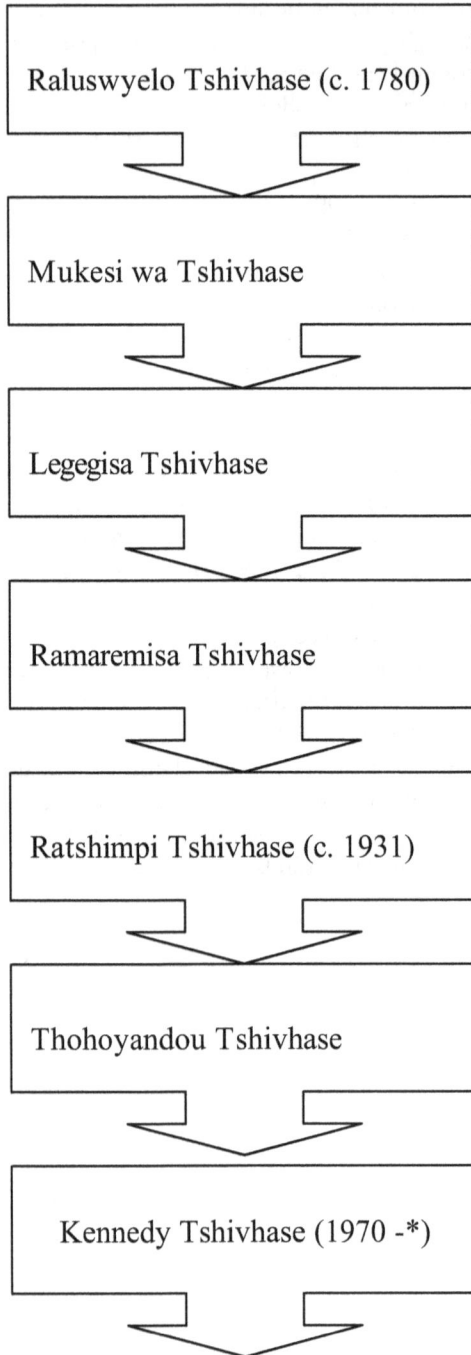

Raluswyelo Tshivhase (c. 1780)

⬇

Mukesi wa Tshivhase

⬇

Legegisa Tshivhase

⬇

Ramaremisa Tshivhase

⬇

Ratshimpi Tshivhase (c. 1931)

⬇

Thohoyandou Tshivhase

⬇

Kennedy Tshivhase (1970 -*)

⬇

Appendix Two

Structure of Traditional Government in Tshivhase

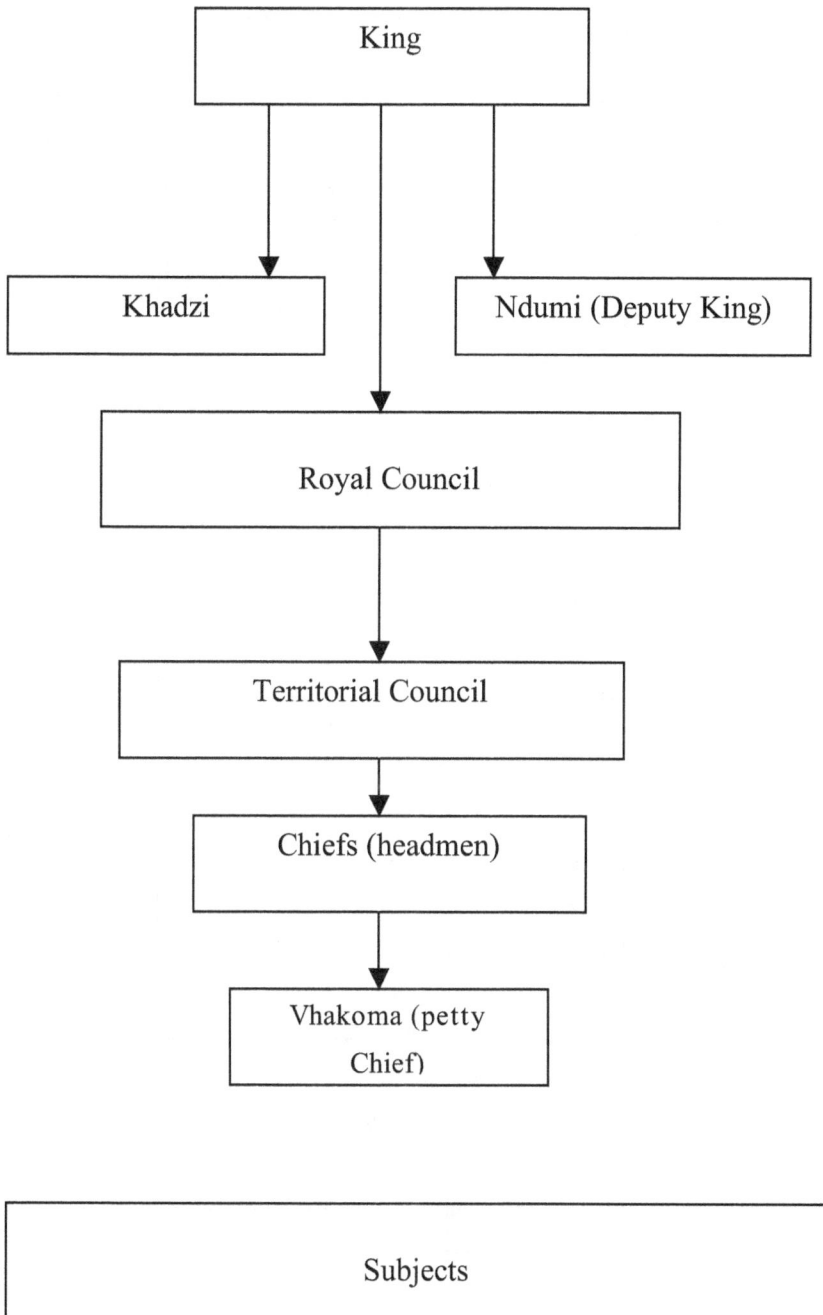

```
                    ┌─────────────────┐
                    │      King       │
                    └─────────────────┘
                       │           │
      ┌──────────┐     │           │   ┌──────────────────────┐
      │  Khadzi  │←────┘           └──→│ Ndumi (Deputy King)  │
      └──────────┘     │               └──────────────────────┘
                       ↓
              ┌────────────────────┐
              │   Royal Council    │
              └────────────────────┘
                       ↓
              ┌────────────────────┐
              │ Territorial Council│
              └────────────────────┘
                       ↓
              ┌────────────────────┐
              │  Chiefs (headmen)  │
              └────────────────────┘
                       ↓
              ┌────────────────────┐
              │  Vhakoma (petty    │
              │      Chief)        │
              └────────────────────┘

              ┌────────────────────────────────┐
              │          Subjects              │
              └────────────────────────────────┘
```

Genealogy of Bali-Nyonga Chiefs

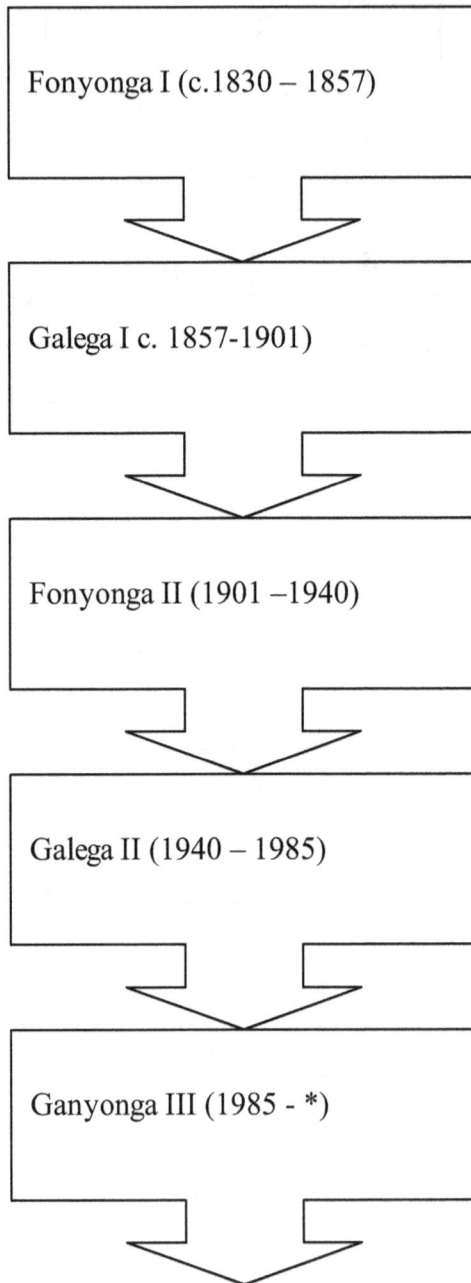

Fonyonga I (c.1830 – 1857)

Galega I c. 1857-1901)

Fonyonga II (1901 –1940)

Galega II (1940 – 1985)

Ganyonga III (1985 - *)

Structure of Traditional Government in Bali-Nyonga

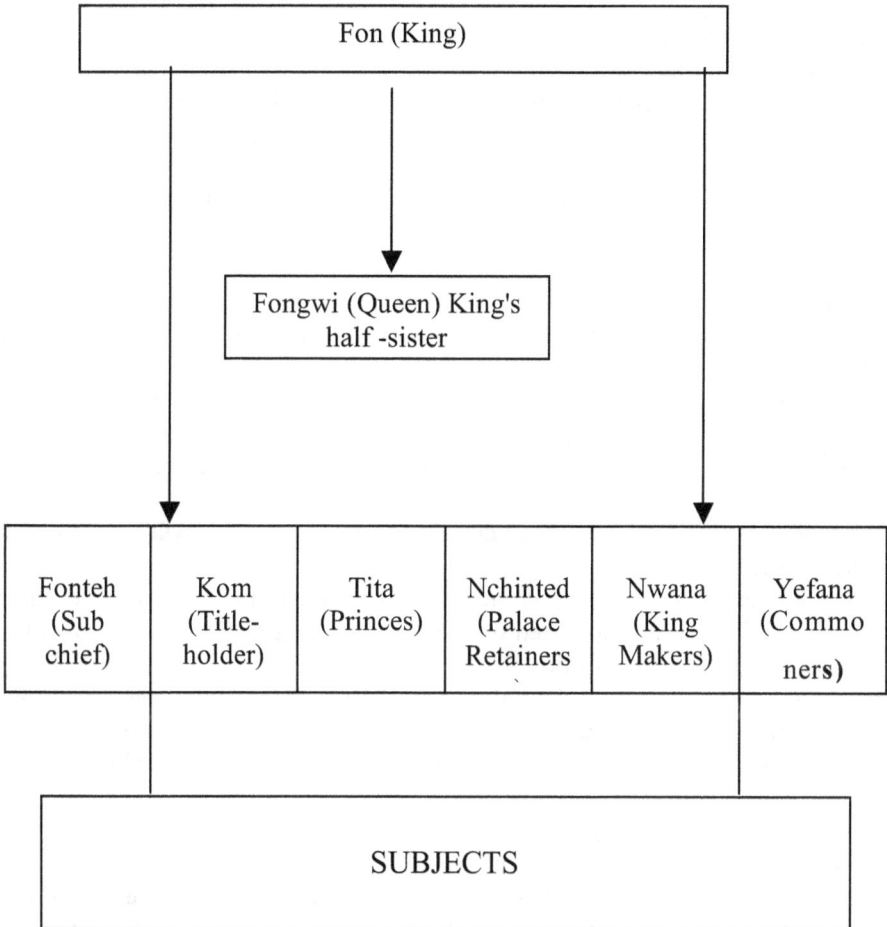

Fon (King)

Fongwi (Queen) King's half -sister

Fonteh (Sub chief)	Kom (Title-holder)	Tita (Princes)	Nchinted (Palace Retainers	Nwana (King Makers)	Yefana (Commo ners)

SUBJECTS

End Notes

[1] Memorandum of the Civics to the Thulamela Municipal Council, August 23, 2001.

[2] This is the popular grassfields word for chief although there are slight variations across the region. In Kom, it is known as *foyn*, in Bafut as *fo'* and in Nso' as *nfor*. I use "fon" as a generic term for chief despite claims in certain circles that it should be used exclusively in reference to first class traditional rulers recognised as such by the national government.

[3] See Statistics South Africa, http://www.statssa.gov.za/census01/html/default.asp . According to the last population census of 2001 and mid-year assessments of 2008 the Tshivhase area has a population count of over a hundred thousand making it the most populated Venda chiefdom.

[4] Fast Facts; South African Institute of Race Relations, No. 2/92, March 1992. P.3

[5] ibid. p. 3

[6] Statistics SA, http://www.statssaa.gov.za

[7] As will be seen in the next chapter, Patrick Mphephu (Venda President from 1979 to1988) allegedly favoured citizens from his own chiefdom over those of rival areas such as Tshivhase, particularly in matters of recruitment into the civil service.

[8] According to the presidential decree of 15 July 1977, defining the role of chiefs and the status of chiefdoms, five chiefdoms in the North West Province were classified as first degree or first class chiefdoms. According to this decree, a 'first class' chiefdom is located within the territorial limits of an administrative division and consists of at least, two sub-chiefs. Details on this decree will be discussed in chapter four.

[9] In the Bamenda grassfields (Bali included), it is believed that a fon never dies. A fon is believed to have disappeared or vanished upon his death. In some chiefdoms, he is said to be 'lost'. In his brief memoir edited by Sally Chilver, Maxwell Fohtung refers to the passing away of the Bali fon in 1940 as the fire that was extinguished. He also notes that each new reign is marked by the lighting of a new fire in the palace which is rapidly distributed to all households in the chiefdom (Fohtung 1992).

[10] Source: http://www.cia.gov/cia/publications/factbook/geos/cm.html#intro

[11] *Le Messager* Vol. II Monday September 14 1992 p. 5

[12] Article 276 (1) of the Constitution states that 'a chief shall not take part in active politics; and any chief wishing to do so and seeking election to Parliament shall abdicate his stool or skin.' Article 94 (3) c) reinforces this by noting that a person shall not be eligible to be a Member of Parliament if he is a chief (Boafo-Arthur 2001).

[13] Other reasons advanced by chiefs in Ghana for abstaining from partisan politics are: chiefs aligning with political parties compromise their roles as the 'fathers of everybody' in their respective communities; chiefs lose their respect when they identify with political parties; although chiefs are by vocation politicians, joining political parties may set them against their subjects who may be members of other political parties; a partisan chief is likely to lose respect if the party he openly identifies with loses power; a non-partisan chief becomes the conscience of the

nation with sufficient moral authority to call politicians to order when matters appear to be getting out of hand (Boafo-Arthur 2001:9-10).

[14] Early ethnographers have observed that one of the major differences between the Vhatavhatsinde and other Venda groups is their method of disposing of the dead. Informants confirmed this practice during my fieldwork but insisted that today it is restricted to royal families. While other groups bury their dead permanently, the Vhatavhatsinde exhume the corpse after several months and burn the bones in a ritual ceremony after which the ashes are scattered in specified rivers.

[15] It is claimed that the Ngona are the original inhabitants of the territory. After their leader was subjugated by the Makhwinde invaders, the Ngona chief became a high priest of the Ngona deity and was frequently invited by their conquerors to serve as a medium between Ngona ancestral spirits and the MaKhwinde invaders.

[16] Loubser (1990) disputes the depiction of this group by some ethnographers as disorganised and primitive. She maintains that this version of history has been projected by invading groups in order to convey the idea that they had a superior technology and were more 'civilised' than the Ngona.

[17] Stayt and others maintain that the death of Dimbanyika is a favourite myth among the Venda. While some accounts hold that Phophi killed his father, others insist that Dimbanyika went hunting in a cave and while he was inside, a rock fell and covered the entrance, thereby entombing him alive.

[18] There is a popular myth among the Tshivhase that the Mphapuli were previously employees of the Tshivhase chief and were entrusted with looking after their cattle. Eventually, the Mphaphuli became very powerful and established their own chiefdom not far from the Tshivhase controlled area. Whereas Stayt (1968) has a different version of how the Mphaphuli kingdom came about, (Ralushai 1979) has disputed this myth in his article, 'The Mphaphuli Dynasty: A Critical Analysis of Oral Sources and Written Accounts concerning the History of the Mphaphuli Dynasty of the Northern Transvaal, South Africa'

[19] See v. d. Heyden (n.d.) 'The Fighting Tradition of the Venda People' for details.

[20] (Heyden n.d.) The author contends that at the end of the 19th century, the Mphaphuli and Tshivhase chiefs 'surrendered to the colonial conquerors without a fight.' He argues further that these chiefs also failed to assist the Mphephu chiefs in their fight against the Boers due to rivalry between them (p.12).

[21] The dispute was based on the claim that Kennedy Tshivhase's mother was not the chosen woman tasked with the "right" to give birth to the heir. In Venda custom, the Makhadzi – i.e. the father's sister reserves the right to choose the future mother of the heir.

[22] See http://www.anc.org.za/anc/newsbrief/1994/news1025 of Tuesday 25 October 1994 in which Tshivhase promises to lodge a land claim with the Northern Transvaal local government and land Ministry in Pietersburg. Chief Patrick Mphephu had incorporated the said land into his territory in 1981.

[23] See www.demarcation.org.za for details. It is possible to interpret the exclusion of the Mphephu chiefdom from the main municipal council in Venda as a form of exclusion in the new democratic dispensation. Besides, the Mphephu chiefs have also been sidelined in the post-apartheid era, as they do not hold similar influential

roles in the ANC like Chief Tshivhase.

[24] Chief Kutama, Chairperson of the Traditional Leaders in Limpopo Province. http://www.zoutnet.co.za/archive/2001/March/2nd/newsmarch2.asp?stoNum=2 1.

[25] Speech by Ngoaka Ramatlhodi, the then Premier of the Limpopo Province, at the Provincial Conference of CONTRALESA on 11 November 2000.

[26] 'The ANC denounces the call by Contralesa President and ANC MP Phatekile Holomisa for a boycott of the local government elections on 1 November. The call has the effect of denying citizens in the rural areas of their right to vote and shape their own future, and is contrary to everything the ANC stands for.' (ANC Press Statement, signed by Cyril Ramaphosa, Secretary General, ANC, 30 October 1995). www.anc.org.za

[27] In this connection the Department of Provincial and Local Government published in October 2002, a *Draft White Paper on Traditional Leadership and Governance*. The final White Paper was published in 2003.

[28] Roca Report No. 133. 1995

[29] Each District Council consists of several municipalities, collectively administered by an Executive Mayor. The Vhembe District Council consists of the Thohoyandou TLC among others.

[30] I use the term development with much caution, bearing in mind that it is somehow elusive. However, the concept was frequently employed by civics to refer to the betterment of their living conditions. To a large extent, job creation epitomised the shared sense of what different individuals referred to or understood as development.

[31] Chief Tshivhase's friend is the son of a German missionary who returned to his birthplace (Venda) after twenty years living in Germany.

[32] Mr. S., Member of the Tshivhase Territorial Council, interviewed on 27 May 2001.

[33] It is important to point out that one of the factors that contributed to less conflict was the change in membership of civic movements. Though I would define most of the members of the civics as youth, it is important to bear in mind that these are not the same youths of the 1980s or early 1990s. Most of the youth I encountered were young teachers in secondary and primary schools, university students who lived in rural areas, traders, policemen, nurses and shopkeepers. Some of them had participated in the activities of the early 1990s, such as the civic leader of Mukumbani who stated that he had taken part in burning a witch. At that time, he remembered vividly, he and other boys of his age were not passionately involved in the activities but simply acted on the instruction of older boys. Some of the current members of the civics groups became active only recently bringing in new ideas and strategies different from those of the struggle era.

[34] Interview with Mr. P, a teacher at the Tshivhase High School, on the 25 June 2001.

[35] *Domba* is an initiation school for girls whose activities have been well documented by anthropologists – see Blacking and Huffman (1985). During Domba, the girls are taught how to be 'proper Venda women'. The ceremony usually ends with their formal graduation to the status of women (cf. Stayt 1968:140).

[36] *Mail and Guardian* of 13 April 2001 pg.8.

[37] See Sechaba ka'Nkosi 'Political Arrogance precludes solutions' *Sunday Times* 06 October 2002 pg. 21 and Devan Pillay 'Between the market and a hard place' in the same edition, pg.24.

[38] The term grasslands or grassfields was first coined by the Germans to describe the Bamenda highlands, which was geographically different from the forest coastal region (Fowler and Zeitlyn 1996).

[39] Fonyonga literally means fon of the Nyonga people.

[40] Zintgraff is alleged to have done two things that angered the Bafut fon. He had seized the drinking cup from the fon's hands and drank from it and he also insisted on calling the fon by his princely name which was considered an abomination. Cf. http://lucy.ukc.ac.uk/Chilver/Paideuma/setting.html

[41] Pact signed between Galega I and Dr. Eugene Zintgraff in August 1891.

[42] Except for Bali Nyonga, most of the Chamba groups in the Bamenda grassfields have retained the original Chamba language known as Mubako. Mungaka emerged from a mixture of Bati and Bamum languages soon after the Chamba split into different factions. Although the royal family retained Mubako for a long time, Mungaka became the dominant language in Bali and subsequently spread to other parts of the grassfields. Mubako is still used in Bali for particular ritual purposes, especially during the Lela festival.

[43] Several German firms had been set up in the coast and needed cheap supply of labour. Previously, these companies recruited labourers from Ghana and Liberia but most of them hardly stayed beyond two years. The Bali chief was expected to supply cheap labour to the coastal plantations in return for colonial protection and expansion of his territory.

[44] The British Government officially assumed effective office in Bamenda in January 1916. The area became known as the Bamenda Division and its first Divisional Officer was Podevin (cf. Nyamndi, 1988:132).

[45] *Confidential Memorandum on the Bali Area,* Bamenda, 3/10/1921.

[46] At this time, the then Cameroons Province as it was known was attached to the Southern Provinces of Nigeria for administrative purposes. The headquarters was in Enugu.

[47] For instance, there were people who felt that unification between a minority English-speaking state and a dominant French-speaking territory was doomed to fail. Chief Dr E M L Endeley was a strong proponent of this view although he changed his mind after reunification in his competition for power against John Ngu Foncha.

[48] In accordance with this decree, five first class chiefdoms were recognised viz; Bafut, Bali, Kom, Mankon and Nso'. The rest were classified as Second or Third class chiefdoms.

49 As the name implies, towns and cities were either deserted or economic activities stopped. Cities were expected to be as calm as a 'grave yard'. During the ghost town period, business activities were limited to Saturdays and Sundays, which permitted people to stock up on groceries needed for the rest of the week. The principal aim of the ghost towns was to weaken the economy and force the Biya regime either into a dialogue with those advocating more democratic reform or to resign.

50 Cf. *Cameroon Post*, Wednesday September 12-19, 1990 pg. 2

51 Angwafor was appointed to replace John Ngu Foncha. Dr Foncha had resigned from his post as vice president of the ruling party for several reasons, one of which was his dissatisfaction with sucessive Francophone-dominated administrations for their oppressive and exploitative treatment of the Anglohpone minority.

52 Recent claims indicate that although the CPDM constitution does not clearly ban chiefs from overt participation in party politics, Paul Biya explicitly objected to their inclusion in the party hierarchy during the reorganisation of party organs in 2002. This claim is cited in the French-language newspaper, *L'Action* which states that: 'Finally, the status of ex-officio member of the executive of a basic organ (Articles 11, 12 and 14 of the Party Constitution) forbids party militants who are 1st and 2nd class chiefs to run for any post whatsoever.' See "Chiefs Should Shun Politics" by Prince Paddy Awonfor, The Post, online edition, http://www.postnewsline.com/2006/11/chiefs_should_s.html, accessed on 11 August 2006.

53 *Cameroon Post* No. 38 Tuesday July 31-August 7, 1990 pg.1

54 *Le Messager* No. 004 of Tuesday August 21 1990 pg.3

55 *Cameroon Tribune* No. 1012 1990 pg.5

56 *The Herald* No. 110 Thursday May 26-29 1994 pg.3

57 *The Herald* No. 574 Friday February 20-22 1998 pg.8

58The Constitution of the Republic of Cameroon (1996), Reproduced by the HURCLED Centre. The constitutional clause that limits presidentail tenures to no more than two terms was lifted by the CPDM-dominated parliament in February 2008 provoking widespread violence in major towns of Cameroon, particularly in Douala and Bamenda where opposition to the proposal was deeply opposed. This constitutional revision is interpreted by many analysts as Biya's attempt to hold on to power after 2011 when his second and final tenure is expected to end.

59 After independence, the Bali Native Authority was transformed to the Bali Area Council. The new council included the chiefdoms of Bali Gham, Bawok and Bosah under the leadership of Galega II. In 1974 a presidential decree reorganised local government in the country. Law No. 74-23 of 5th December 1974 stipulated that the municipal council shall be headed by a municipal administrator appointed by the state. Although legislation governing the operation of local government in Cameroon has been modified since 1990, it still owes much to the 1972 decree.

60 *The Herald* No. 275, Thursday, 11-14 January. It was also reported that after the fon's defeat at the polls, some subjects called on him to resign based on allegations that he had threatened to resign if his subjects failed to vote him into office. *The Herald* No. 281, Friday, 02-04 February, 1996. Pg.3.

[61] In Bali, it is customary to celebrate the death of deceased relatives soon after their burial. It is believed that failure to do so may invoke the wrath of the ancestors on the living.

[62] Interview with a CPDM militant and supporter of the fon, at the D.O.'s Office Bali, 10 February 2001.

[63] Interview with fon Ganyonga at his palace in Bali on 20 February 2002.

[64] The late fon of Nso, Nga II seems to have captured this viewpoint explicitly when he issued a letter to all the subjects of his chiefdom stating that: 'as the Fon of all of you, I have welcomed all shades of political opinion. It has been a most uncomfortable experience for me to observe a split between many a traditional ruler and his people because of political difference. Our history as far as the Fondom is concerned – from our various clichés and proverbs and the role of the Fon – shows that the occupant of the Stool must be non-partisan. I have striven to be so even though this still has not gained the admiration of all of you.' *Le Messager* Vol. II No. 37 Saturday, October 10, 1992 p.12).

[65] Interviewed at Jam Jam, Bali, 5th January 2002.

[66] The SDF has consistently branded itself as a national party as opposed to an Anglophone party. In this regard, it has succeeded to attract a number of Francophone supporters especially from the Western and Littoral provinces. Although members of the SDF may belong to different Anglophone lobby groups, their focus is on winning national influence as opposed to representing the Anglophone cause. Because of its failure to privilege the Anglophone cause, some opinion leaders like Boniface Forbin, the publisher of The Herald newspaper, have begun to advocate quite strongly, the need for an Anglophone political party (The Herald 21 October 2001, www.heraldnewspaper.net). In fact, his advocacy in this regard materialised following his creation of a party in 2004 which has remained largely unknown or inactive.

[67] See http://web.amnesty.org/report2005/cmr-summary-eng

[68] Ganyonga has refuted these accusations. He maintained that: 'unfortunately, people have a very wrong image of the Balis, especially here in the North West. Contrary to that opinion we are not aggressive and we are not expansionist. The Balis have their boundaries established since 1954, and since my installation I have never instructed my people to go beyond our boundaries because we are not claiming even an inch of anybody's land.' *The Herald* No. 214, Monday June 19-21, 1995 pg.6.

[69] *The Herald* No. 214, Monday June 19-21, 1995 pg. 6

[70] http://groups.yahoo.com/groups/mbonbani

[71] Account Statement of BANDECA as posted on its discussion group: http://groups.yahoo.com/groups/mbonbani

[72] *The Herald* No. 1072 Monday, 25-26 June 2001. Pg. 7

[73] 'We are not a political party, but the Fons as individuals have the right to militate (sic) in any political party of their choice. The Union cannot declare itself for the SDF, CPDM, UPC etc. *But this does not mean the Union is insensitive to political issues.*' (Emphasis mine). Fon Abumbi, Leader of the North West Fon's Union in an interview with *The Herald* No. 658 Wednesday September 9-10, 1998 pg. 9.

[74]*The Herald* No. 243 Thursday, September21-24 1995. Pg.1

[75] *The Herald* No. 231, Monday August 17-19, 1995, pg.1

[76] *The Herald* No. 641 Monday, August 3-4, 1998. Pg. 2

[77] SDF Parliamentarian for Menchum Division, *The Herald* No. 656 Friday, September 4-6 1998 pg.3.

[78] *The Herald* No. 625 Friday, June 26-28, 1998 pg. 3.

[79] See The Post, online edition titled "Lifting of Fon Doh's Immunity: The Inside Story of a Great Fall" http://www.postnewsline.com/2005/02/stronglifting_o.html accessed on 24 February 2005.

[80] See The Post, online edition, "Doh Gah Gwanyin Found Guilty!" http://www.postnewsline.com/2006/04/doh_gah_gwanyin.html accessed on 10 June 2006.

[81] See The Post online edition, "Justice Minister Says Fon Doh Is Not A Convict". During a question session at the National Assembly, an SDF MP asked the Minister of Justice why fon Doh who had been convicted and sentenced for 15 years was instead living as a free man. The Minister responded that fon Doh was not a convict and in fact that he was still earning his salary as MP. See http://www.postnewsline.com/2006/12/justice_ministe.html, accessed on 15 January 2007.

[82] See The Post accessed through the Allafrica.com news service, "Nowefu Meeting - Ntumfor/Fon Chafah Conflict Takes Centre Stage" http://allafrica.com/stories/printable/200808190185.html accessed on 15 September 2008.

[83] See The Post online edition, "Suspension of Barrister Ntumfor Nico Halle". http://www.postnewsline.com/2008/08/press-releasesu.html accessed on 30 September 2008. The Press release suspending the ntumfor accuses him of "attempts to destabilise and destroy the Fons' union, through persistent, reckless and unfounded press declarations."

[84] See The Post, online edition, "Chafah/Ntumfor Imbroglio Blamed On Pride", http://www.postnewsline.com/2008/09/chafahntumfor-i.html accessed on 5 October 2008.

[85] After the presidential election of 1997, a group of fons visited the presidency to express their support for Paul Biya and to lobby for more posts for their subjects. See *The Herald* No. 528 Friday, October 31 - November 2, 1997 pg.1-2.

[86] During Prime Minister Peter Musonge's visit to Bamenda in April 2001, the fons of the North West Province conferred the title of *achendum* or 'Pathfinder' to him. In an elaborate address during the ceremony, the Secretary General of NOWEFU urged the visiting PM to 'Tell the president that we the North West province with one voice assure him that the province is a ripen fruit waiting for him to come and harvest.' Fon Chafah, the Secretary General of NOWEFU in his address to the Prime minister on 4th April 2001. See *The Herald* No. 1040 Friday 6-8 April 2001 pg. 3.

87 An excerpt of the Declaration reads: 'As a people, our common values, vision, and goals and those of our Francophone partners in the Union are different, and clearly can not harmonise within the framework of a Unitary State such as was imposed on us in 1972. The democratic principle of majority rule and minority rights leads us to believe in the rights and freedoms of the minority. Francophone Regimes who have lead (sic) this country, have pursued a policy of assimilation aimed at wiping out our identity. Thus, our vision of a bicultural society becomes illusive, unattainable goals, and will remain so until and unless we can find a better framework within which this aspiration can find expression.'

88 An Address presented by the North West Fons on the occasion of the All Anglophones Conference holding in Buea South West Province, 2nd April 1993; *Cameroon Post Special* No. 157 April 17 pg. 16.

89 *The Messenger* Vol 1. No. 003 Thursday May 13, 1993 pg. 5

90 A Welcome Address presented by Opinion Leaders, Elderly Statesmen and Natural Rulers in Bamenda to His Exellency Chief Emeka Anyaoku. *Cameroon Post* No. 170 June 1993 pg. 5.

91 *The Herald* No. 237, Monday September 4-6, 1995 pg. 1-2.

92 *The Herald* No. 1161 Monday 28-29 January 2002 pg. 2.

93 SCNC Press Release on 3rd October 2002 at Bamenda.

94 The fons included Abumbi II of Bafut who was the then chairman of the North West Fons' Union (NOWEFU), fon Angwafor of Mankon, Sehm Mbinglo of Nso, Vincent Yuh I of Kom and fon Doh Gayonga III of Bali. The fons were accompanied by their *ntumfor* (ambassador), Barrister Nico Halle. See *The Herald* of 21st October 2002. Cf. www.heraldnewspaper.net

95 See *The Herald* of 23rd October 2002 - 'Three Cheers to Anglophone Chiefs' in which the fons' trip to the presidency is perceived as a heroic gesture. But a word of caution is offered specifically that any Anglophone leaders willing to fight the cause should be ready to fight to the end, although it is not clear what end is envisaged or who defines the end.

96 The Lela festival is an annual cultural event that celebrates the end of the year and the beginning of a new one. Usually held in December for a period of four days, the festival is characterised by traditional sacrifices to the ancestors, led by the fon. It is also a period during which the Bali people commemorate the achievements of the past year and pray for a better and prosperous New Year. In summary, the Lela festival constitutes the meeting point of all Bali members at home and abroad, by affirming the unity of the clan and the central role of the 'fon as father of all'. See Richard Fardon's (2006) work on the Lela festival.

97 The traditional council has changed significantly not only in terms of its membership but also in its functions. Originally, it consisted of the seven permanent notables (kom kwatat) whose positions were hereditary, the sub-chiefs (fonte) and palace retainers. During the reign of Galega II the traditional council was broadened to include other sub-groups in Bali society such as the royal children and the king-makers. Ganyonga is the first fon to have appointed a woman into the council.

98 Interview with the Vice President of the Traditional Council at Njenka, Bali. 20 February 2002.

99 Interview with a female informant at Tikali, 20th December 2001.

100 *Cameroon Post*, No. 0125 Monday 14 September 1996 pg. 12.

101 The CPDM won the mayoral office from the SDF following the municipal election of July 2007 largely because the SDF's list was rejected by the government-controlled body charged with organising elections.

102 *Mail & Guardian May* 31-June 6 2000, Blacksash Advertisement.

103 The present Chief Mphephu belongs to the United Democratic Movement (UDM) led by Bantu Holomisa. This party is relatively insignificant in the Limpopo Province where the ANC is indeed the only game in town.

104 These mechanisms and institutions consist of universal suffrage based on proportional representation, national and local or regional legislatures; multiplicity of political parties, an autonomous constitutional court, several commissions protecting different kinds of rights etc. See Tom Lodge's *South African Politics Since 1994*.

105 Chief P. Holomisa in the *Mail and Guardian* of 11 February 2000: "*Ubukhosi*, the bedrock of African Democracy."

106 'The institution of traditional leadership has an important and integral part to play in the building of our new Constitutional order. Traditional leaders have a particular role to play as custodians of culture and custom, the promotion of unity, the promotion of consensus around development projects and plans and the administration of justice in democratically transformed courts.' ANC Mafikeng Conference resolution on traditional leadership (1997).

107 The November issue of *New African* (No. 412) carried a special cover story on the land issue in South Africa. It suggested that the land issue in South Africa is a ticking time bomb and that so far, the government has failed in meeting its objectives as stipulated in 1994.

108 Government Gazette of 01 October 1991.

109 In 1998 Chief Netshimbufe (a headman in Tshivhase) was arrested and jailed for a week because he held a court session to discuss a witchcraft-related dispute. The supposed victim of the witchcraft attack was reported to have consulted a diviner who revealed that Mr K. was the wizard responsible for his misfortune. After hearing about the accusation, Mr K promptly reported the chief and his accuser to the police and were arrested. Even though this incident frightened both chiefs and subjects for a while, I was informed that many still report criminal offences to their headmen.

110 Cameroon's transition has been described as a 'passive revolution' for various reasons. It has been argued that although this transition was minimal, it created political space for individual and collective action. This led to the proliferation of pressure groups and consequently, more capacity for civil society to engage in different kinds of political action (cf. Sindjoun, 1999:4).

111 This may no longer be the case given the arrest of many high-profile CPDM officials accused of embezzling government funds. Membership in the CPDM no longer seems to grant immunity to officials, a trend that has left many questioning the usefulness of CPDM membership. In the North West Province for example, the accusation and arrest of Zaccheus Forjindam, an influential member of the CPDM

in the province and formerly director of the Cameroon shipyard Company, a government parastatal – has left many members disillusioned and anxious. See The Post, "Alleged Plot to Kill Forjindam Unveiled", http://allafrica.com/stories/200810241036.html, posted to the internet on 24 October 2008 and accessed on 28 October 2008.

[112] Bratton and Van de Walle (1997) have contended that the success that was achieved in many African countries between 1990 and 1992 has either been reversed or is eroding. According to them, Cameroon's transition efforts could be described as 'survival' intermediately located between a 'reversal to authoritarianism' and 'the difficult process of consolidation' (Bratton and Van de Walle 1997:235).

[113] Following preparations for the legislative and local government elections in 2002, several key members of the party were reported to have resigned in protest of the dictatorial nature of the party chairman and his allies. Rigging and irregularities were also reported to have marred the SDF primary elections in many parts of the North West Province (*The Herald* No. 1201, 10 May 2002). Further infighting in 2005 led to the resignation of its secretary general as well as other high profile office holders.

[114] http://www.electionworld.org/election/cameroon.htm accessed on the 28th December 2002.

[115] www.crtv.cm of 01/10/2002. In his assessment of the June 30 elections, Tankwa Claude, the online editor of CRTV suggested a number of reasons why the CPDM registered a massive victory. Among the reasons, he noted that some 'senior divisional officers did all in their power to ground the opposition. This was seen at the level of voter registration, the distribution of voter's cards and the management of election results.'

[116] I make use of the concept of performance as elaborated by (Goffman 1959). In this context, the observers are expected to believe that the tasks performed by the actor 'are what they appear to be.' However, the actor may or may not be fully taken in by his own act (Goffman 1959:28-29).

[117] *Cameroon Post* Monday June 16 1997 pg. 11.

[118] *Herald* No. 476 Wednesday, June 25-26, 1997 pg. 5.

[119] Patrick Chabal, 1996. 'The African Crisis: Context and Interpretation' in Richard Werbner and Terence Ranger (eds.) *Postcolonial Identities in Africa.*

[120] Chapter 12 of the 1996 Constitution recognises the role of chiefs over customary practices. Though it does not define tradition, it is taken here as a set of practices handed down from one generation to another and believed to be unchanging even when the contrary is true.

[121] See for example the appointment in 2002 of a minister of Nso origin, allegedly on recommendation by the Fon of Nso. Similar claims have been made about Ganyonga's influence in the appointment of Bali elite to positions of prominence in Cameroon.

References

Ake, Claude. 2000. *The Feasibility of Democracy in Africa.* Dakar: CODESRIA.

Amin, Samir. 1994. The Issue of Democracy in the Contemporary Third World. In *African Perspectives on Development: Controversies, Dilemmas, and Openings*, edited by Ulf Himmelstrand et al. London: James Currey.

Anderson, Benedict. 1991. *Imagined Communities: Reflections on the Origin and Spread of Nationalism.* London: Verso.

Atanga, Mufor L. 1994. The Political Economy of West Cameroon: A Study in the Alienation of a Linguistic Minority. M.Sc. Thesis, Ahmadou Bello University, Zaria.

Bali-Nyonga History and Culture Committee. 1986. *History of the Bali Family.* Bamenda: Radio Cameroon.

Bank, Leslie , and Roger Southall. 1996. Traditional Leaders in South Africa's New Democracy. *Journal of Legal Pluralism* 37-38:407-430.

Barrett, S. R. 1996. *Anthropology : A Student's Guide to Theory and Method.* Toronto: University of Toronto Press.

Bayart, J-F. 1989. *L'État en Afrique: La Politique du Ventre.* Paris: Fayard.

Bayart, J-F., Stephen Ellis, and B. Hibou. 1999. *The Criminalization of the State in Africa.* Oxford: James Currey.

Bayart, J.-F, P. Geschiere, and F. B. Nyamnjoh. 2001. Autochtonie, démocratie et citoyenneté en Afrique. *Critique Internationale* 10:177-194.

Becker, Heike. 2006. "New Things after Independence": Gender and Traditional Authorities in Postcolonial Namibia. *Journal of Southern African Studies* 32 (1):29 - 48.

BERCD. 1979. *The Independent Venda.* Pretoria: Benso.

Blacking, John, and Thomas N. Huffman. 1985. The Great Enclosure and Domba. *Man* 20 (3):542-545.

Boafo-Arthur, Kwame. 2001. Chieftaincy and Politics in Ghana Since 1982. *West Africa Review* 3 (1).

Bourdieu, Pierre. 1977. *Outline of a Theory of Practice.* Cambridge: Cambridge University Press.

Bratton, M. , and Nicolas Van de Valle. 1997. *Democratic Experiments in Africa: Regime Transition in Comparative Perspective.* Cambridge: Cambridge University Press.

Chabal, Patrick. 1996. The African Crisis: Context and Interpretation. In *Postcolonial Identities in Africa*, edited by R. Werbner and T. Ranger. London: Zed Books.

Chem-Langhëë, Bongfen. 2004. *The Paradoxes of Self-determination in the Cameroons under United Kingdom Administration: The Search for Identity, Well-being and Continuity.* Lanham, MD: University Press of America.

Chiabi, Emmanuel. 1997. *The Making of Modern Cameroon: A History of Substate Nationalism and Disparate Union, 1914-1961.* Lanham, MD: University Press of America.

Chilver, E. M., and Phyllis Kaberry. 1967. *Traditional Bamenda: The Precolonial History and Ethnography of the Bamenda Grassfields.* Buea, Cameroon: Government Printer.

Comaroff, J., and J. L. Comaroff. 1999a. Alien-Nation: Zombies, Immigrants, and Millenial Capitalism. *Codesria Bulletin* 3 & 4:17-28.

————. 1999b. Occult Economies and the violence of abstraction: notes from the South African postcolony. *American Ethnologist* 26 (2):279-301.

————. 2000. Millenial Capitalism: First Thoughts on a Second Coming. *Public Culture* 12 (2):291-343.

Commey, P. 2002. Land: South Africa's ticking time Bomb. *New African*, November 2002, 12-16.

Deegan, H. 1999. *South Africa Reborn: Building a new democracy*. London: UCL Press.

Delius, Peter. 1996. *A Lion Amongst the Cattle: Reconstruction and Resistance in the Northern Transvaal*. Johannesburg: Ravan Press.

Department of Provincial and Local Government. 2002. *Draft White Paper on Traditional Leadership and Governance*. Pretoria, South Africa.

Du Plessis, W., and Theo Scheepers. 1999. House of Traditional Leaders: Role, Problems and Future. Paper read at Constitution and the Law, at Potchesfstroom, South Africa.

Eyoh, Dickson. 1998a. Conflicting narratives of Anglophone protest and the politics of identity in Cameroon. *Journal of Contemporary African Studies* 16:249-276.

————. 1998b. Through the prism of a local tragedy: Political liberasation, regionalism and elite struggles for power in Cameroon. *Africa* 68:338-359.

————. 2004. Contesting Local Cititizenship: Liberalization and the Politics of Difference in Cameroon. In *Ethnicity and Democracy in Africa*, edited by B. Berman, D. Eyoh and W. Kymlicka. Oxford & Athens, OH: James Currey & Ohio University.

Eyongetah, R., and Robert Brain. 1974. *A History of the Cameroon*. London: Longman.

Fanthorpe, Richard. 2005. On the limits of liberal peace: Chiefs and democratic decentralization in post-war Sierra Leone. *African Affairs* 104 (418):27-49.

Fardon, Richard. 2006. *Lela in Bali: History through Ceremony in Cameroon*. Oxford: Berghahn Books.

Fisiy, Cyprian F. 1995. Chieftaincy in the modern state: an institution at the crossroads of democratic change. *Paideuma* 41:49-62.

Fohtung, Maxwell Gabana. 1992. Self-portrait of a Cameroonian. *Paideuma* 38:219-248.

Fowler, I., and D. Zeitlyn. 1996. The Grassfields and the Tikar. In *African Crossroads: Intersections between history and Anthropology in Cameroon*, edited by I. Fowler and D. Zeitlyn. Providence and Oxford: Berghahn Books.

Friedman, John T. 2005. Making Politics, Making History: Chiefship and the Post-Apartheid State in Namibia. *Journal of Southern African Studies* 31 (1):23 - 52.

Gabriel, Jürg Martin. 1999. Cameroon's Neopatrimonial Dilemma. *Journal of Contemporary African Studies* 17 (2):173-196.

Geschiere, P., and Piet Konings, eds. 1993. *Pathways to Accumulation in Cameroon*. Paris and Leiden: African Studies Centre and Karthala.

Geschiere, Peter. 1993. Chiefs and Colonial Rule in Cameroon: Inventing Chieftaincy, French and British Style. *Africa* 63 (2):151-75.

Geschiere, Peter, and Francis B. Nyamnjoh. 2000. Capitalism and Autochthony: The Seesaw of Mobility and Belonging. *Public Culture* 12:423-452.

Giddens, Anthony. 2001. *Sociology*. 4th ed. Cambridge: Polity Press.

Gluckman, Max. 1940. Analysis of a social situation in modern Zululand. *Bantu Studies* 14:1-30.

———. 1963. *Order and Rebellion in Tribal Africa*. London: Cohen.

Goffman, Erving. 1959. *The Presentation of Self in Everyday Life*. Middlesex: The Penguin Press.

Goheen, Miriam. 1992. Chiefs, Sub-chiefs and Local control: Negotiations over Land, Struggles over Meaning. *Africa* 62 (3):389-412.

Gonçalves, Euclides. 2005. Finding the Chief: Political Decentralisation and Traditional Authority in Mocumbi, Southern Mozambique. *Africa Insight* 35 (3):64-70.

Gwellem, J. F. 1996. *Fru Ndi and the SDF Revolution*. Bamenda: Unique Printers.

Hannerz, U. 1997. Borders. *International Social Science Journal* 154/1997:537-547.

Heyden, v.d. U. n.d. *The Fighting Tradition of the Venda People*: Publisher Unknown.

Holland, Dorothy, and Kevin Leander. 2004. Ethnographic Studies of Positioning and Subjectivity: An Introduction. *Ethos* 32 (2):127-139.

Houston, G. 1999. *The National Liberation Struggle in South Africa: A Case Study of the United Democratic Front, 1983-1987*. London: Ashgate.

Hunt, W. E. 1925. *Assessment Report on the Bali Clan of the Bamenda Division, Cameroons Province*. Buea: Buea Archives.

Hyden, Goran, and Michael Bratton, eds. 1992. *Governance and Politics in Africa*. London: Lynne Rienner Publishers.

Jua, N. 1993. State, Oil and Accumulation. In *Pathways to Accumulation in Cameroon*, edited by P. Geschiere and P. Konings. Paris: Karthala.

———. 1995. Indirect Rule in Colonial and Postcolonial Cameroon. *Paideuma* 41:39-47.

Kaberry, P. M., and E. M. Chilver. 1961. An Outline of the Traditional Political System of Bali-Nyonga, Southern Cameroons. *Africa: Journal of the International African Institute* 31 (4):355-371.

Konings, Piet, and F. B. Nyamnjoh. 1997. The anglophone problem in Cameroon. *Journal of Modern African Studies* 35 (2):207-29.

Konings, Piet, and Francis B. Nyamnjoh. 2003. *Negotiating an Anglophone Identity: A Study of the Politics of Recognition and Representation in Cameroon*. Leiden & Boston: Brill.

Lindstrom, L., and Geoffrey White. 1997. *Chiefs Today: Traditional Pacific Leadership and the Postcolonial State*. Stanford: Stanford University Press.

Lodge, T. 1999. *South African Politics since 1994*. Cape Town: David Philip.

Loubser, J. 1990. Oral Traditions, Archaeology and the History of the Mitupo. *African Studies* 49 (2):13-42.

Maloka, E. 1995. Traditional Leaders and the Current Transition. *The African Communist* Second Quarter:35-43.

Maloka, T. 1996. Populism and the Politics of Chieftaincy and Nation-building in the New South Africa. *Journal of Contemporary African Studies* 14 (2):173-196.

Mamdani, Mahmood. 1996. *Citizen and Subject: Contemporary Africa and the Legacy of Late Colonialism*. Princeton, NJ: Princeton University Press.

Marcus, G. E. 1995. Ethnography in/of the world system: the emergence of multi-sited ethnography. *Annual Review of Anthropology* 24:95-117.

Mashele, Prince. 2004. Traditional Leadership in South Africa's New Democracy. *Review of African Political Economy* 31 (100):349-354.

Matshidze, P. E. 2003. *The Universal Church and Pentecostalism in Venda*. MA Thesis, Department of Sociology and Social Anthropology, MA Thesis, University of Stellenbosch, Stellenbosch.

Mbaku, J. M. 2002. Cameroon's Stalled Transition to Democratic Governance: Lessons for Africa's New Democrats. *African and Asian Studies* 1 (3):125-163.

Mbaku, John Mukum, and Joseph Takougang, eds. 2004. *The leadership challenge in Africa : Cameroon under Paul Biya*. Trenton, N.J.: Africa World Press.

Mbeki, Govan. 1984. *The Peasants Revolt*. London: Defence and Aid Fund.

Mbembe, Achille. 1992. Provisional Notes on the Postcolony. *Africa* 62 (1):3-37.

Ministry for Provincial Affairs and Constitutional Development. 1998. *The White Paper on Local Government*. Pretoria, South Africa.

Mudimbe, V. Y. 1988. *The Invention of Africa: Gnosis, Philosophy and the Order of Knowledge*. London: James Currey.

Mukong, Albert, ed. 1990. *The Case for the Southern Cameroons*. Enugu: Chuka Printing Company Ltd.

Nkuna, J. K. 2002. *Local Meanings of Development: The Government, the chief and the Community in Rural Tzaneen*. MA Thesis, Department of Social Anthropology, MA Thesis, University of the Witwatersrand, Johannesburg.

Ntsebeza, L. 1998. Rural Local Government in post-apartheid South Africa. *African Sociological Review* 2 (1):153-164.

Ntsebeza, Lungisile. 2005. *Democracy Compromised: Chiefs and the Politics of the Land in South Africa*. Leiden and Boston: Brill.

Nyamndi, N. B. 1988. *The Bali Chamba of Cameroon: A Political History*. Paris: CAPE.

Nyamnjoh, F. B. 1999. Cameroon: a country united by ethnic ambition and difference. *African Affairs* 98 (390):101-118.

———. 2002a. Cameroon: Over Twelves Years of Comestic Democracy. *Nordic Africa Institute Bulletin* 3 (02).

———. 2002b. "A Child is One Person's Only in the Womb": Domestication, Agency and Subjectivity in the Cameroonian Grassfields. In *Postcolonial Subjectivities in Africa*, edited by R. Werbner. London: Zed Books.

Nyamnjoh, F. B., and Michael Rowlands. 1998. Elite Associations and the politics of Belonging in Cameroon. *Africa* 68 (3):320-37.

Nyamnjoh, Francis B. 2000. "For Many are Called but few are Chosen": Globalisation and Popular Disenchantment in Africa. *African Sociological Review* 4 (2):1-45.

———. 2002c. Might and Right: Chieftaincy and Democracy in Cameroon and Botswana. MS.

O'neil, Robert. 1996. Imperialisms at the Century's End: Moghamo Relationships with Bali-Nyonga and Germany 1889-1908. In *African Crossroads: Intersections between History and Anthropology in Cameroon*, edited by I. Fowler and D. Zeitlyn. Providence and Oxford: Berghahn Books.

Oluwu, D. 1999. Local Governance, Democracy and Develpoment. In *State, Conflict and Democracy in Africa*, edited by R. Joseph. London: Lynne Rienner Publishers.

Oomen, Barbara. 2000. 'We must now go back to our history': Retraditionalisation in a Northern province Chieftaincy. *African Studies* 59 (1).

———. 2002. Chiefs! Law, Power and Culture in Contemporary South Africa. PhD Thesis, University of Leiden, PhD Thesis.

———. 2005. *Chiefs in South Africa: Law, Power and Culture in the Post-Apartheid Era.* Oxford: James Currey.

Ortner, Sherry. 1984. Theory in Anthropology since the Sixties. *Comparative Studies in Society and History.*

Paine, Thomas. 1995. *Rights of Man, Common Sense and Other Political Writings.* Oxford: Oxford University Press.

Radcliffe-Brown, A. R. 1958. *Method in Social Anthropology: Selected Essays by A.R. Radcliffe-Brown.* Edited by e. b. M. N. Srinivas. Chicago: University of Chicago Press.

Ralushai Commisssion. 1996. *Report of the Commission of Inquiry into Witchcraft Violence and Ritual Murders in the Northern Province of the Republic of South Africa.* Pietersburg: The Commission.

Ralushai, Victor. 1977. *Conflicting Accounts of Venda History with Particular Reference to the Role of the Mutupo in the Social Organisation.* PhD Thesis, Queens University, Belfast.

———. 1979. *The Mphaphuli Dynasty: A Critical Analysis of Oral Sources and Written Accounts Concerning the History of the Mpahphuli Dynasty of the Northern Transvaal, South Africa.* Seminar Paper ed. Jos: Jos University, Plateau State, Nigeria.

———. 1980. *Venda History as Presented in Written Works - A Reappraisal.* Venda.

Rowlands, Michael, and J. P. Warnier. 1988. Sorcery, Power and the Modern State in Cameroon. *Man* 23 (1):118-32.

Sandbrook, R. 1988. Liberal Democracy in Africa: A Socialist-revisionist perspective. *Journal of African Studies* 22 (2).

Schapera, I. 1970. *Tribal Innovators: Tswana Chiefs and Social Change 1795-1940.* London: Athlone Press.

Schatzberg, Michael. 1993. Power, Legitimacy, and Democratisation in Africa. *Africa* 63 (4):445-461.

Sharp, J., and Emile Boonzaier. 1994. Ethnic Identity as Performance: Lessons from Namqualand. *Journal of Southern African Studies* 20 (3):405-515.

Sindjoun, L. 1999. Présentation Générale: Éléments pour une Problématique de la Révolution Passive. In *La Révolution Passive au Cameroun: État, Société et Changement*, edited by L. Sindjoun. Dakar: CODESRIA.

Sklar, R. 1986. Democracy in Africa. In *Political Domination in Africa: Reflections on the Limits of Power*, edited by P. Chabal. Cambridge: Cambridge University Press.

South Arican Institute of Race Relations. 1987-1988. Race Relations Survey. Johannesburg.

Stayt, H. 1968. *The BaVenda.* London: Frank Cass and Company Ltd.

The Republic of South Africa. 1996. *The Constitution of the Republic of South Africa.* Act 108 of 1996.

Thornton, R. 2002. *'Traditional Authority' and Governance in the Emjindini Royal Swazi chiefdom, Barberton, Mpumalanga: An Empirical Study*: Unpublished.

Titanji, Vincent, Mathew Gwanfogbe, Elias Nwana, G. Ndangam, and A. S. Lima. 1988. *Introduction to the study of Bali-Nyonga: A Tribute to his Royal Highness Galega II, Traditional Ruler of Bali-Nyonga From 1940-1985*. Bamenda: Stardust Printers.

van Kessel, I, and B Oomen. 1997. 'One chief, one vote': the revival of traditional authorities in post-apartheid South Africa. *African Affairs* 96 (385):561-585.

van Kessel, I. 2000. *'Beyond our Wildest dreams': The United Democratic Front and the Transformation of South Africa*. Charlottesville: University Press of Virginia.

von Trotha, T. 1996. From Administrative to Civil Chieftaincy: Some Problems and Prospects of African Chieftaincy. *Joural of Legal Pluralism* 37-38:79-107.

Warnier, Jean-Pierre. 1993. The King as a Container in the Cameroon Grassfields. *Paideuma* 39:303-19.

West, H G, and S Kloeck-Jenson. 1999. Betwixt and between: 'traditional authority' and democratic decentralization in post-war Mozambique. *African Affairs* 98 (393):455-484.

Zuma, Thando. 1990. The Role of the Chiefs in the Struggle for Liberation' in: African Communist. *African Communist* 121:65-76.

Newspapers

Cameroon Post No. 0191 Wednesday, November 24 – December 1, 1993, pg.2
Cameroon Post No. 170 June 4 1993, pg. 5
Cameroon Post Special No. 157 April 17 pg.16 1993
Cameroon Post, No. 0125 Monday 14 September, 1996 pg. 12
Cameroon Post, No. 38 Tuesday, July 31 – 7 August, 1990 pg.1
Cameroon Post, Wednesday, September 12-19, 1990, pg.2
Cameroon Tribune, No. 1012 1990. pg.5
Confidential Memorandum on the Bali Area, Bamenda, 3/10/1921
Fast Facts, South African Institute of Race Relations, No. 2/92, March 1992 p.3
Le Messager No. 004, Tuesday, August 21 1990, pg.3
Le Messager Vol. II Monday September 14 1992 p.5
Le Messager Vol. II No. 37 Saturday, October 10, 1992 pg.12
Mail and Guardian, 13 April 2001 pg. 8
Mail and Guardian, May 31 – June 6 2000, pg. 10
Roca Report. No. 133 1995.
SCNC Press Release, 3 October 2002, Bamenda.
Sunday Times, 6 October 2002, pp. 21, 24.
The Herald No. 1040 Friday 6 – 8 April 2001, pg. 3
The Herald No. 1072 Monday, 25-26 June 2001. pg.7
The Herald No. 1161, Monday 28 – 29 January 2002 pg.2
The Herald No. 214, Monday June 19-21, 1995 pg.6
The Herald No. 237 4 – 6 September, 1995 pg. 1 – 2
The Herald No. 243 Thursday, September 21-24 1995, pg.1
The Herald No. 275 Thursday, January 11-14 1996 pg.4
The Herald No. 281, Friday, February 02-04, 1996 pg.3
The Herald No. 528 Friday, October 31 – November 2, 1997 pg. 1- 2.
The Herald No. 574 Friday, February 20-22 1998 pg.8

The Herald No. 625 Friday, June 26 – 28 1998, pg. 3
The Herald No. 641 Monday, August 3-4, 1998, pg. 2
The Herald No. 656 Friday, September 4- 6 1998, pg. 3
The Herald, No. 110, Thursday May 26-29 1994, pg.3
The Messenger Vol I. No. 003 Thursday May 13, 1993, pg. 5

Web sites consulted

http://www.statssa.gov.za
http://www.cia.gov/cia/publications/factbook/geos/cm.html#/intro
http://www.mg.co.za .
http://www.anc.org.za/anc/newsbrief/1994/news1025
http://www.demarcation.org.za
http://www.zoutnet.co.za/archive/2001/March/2nd/newsmarch2.asp?stoNum=21
http://www.lucy.ukc.ac.uk/chilver/paideuma/setting.html
http://www.heraldnewspaper.net
http://groups.yahoo.com/groups/mbonbani

www.ingramcontent.com/pod-product-compliance
Lightning Source LLC
Chambersburg PA
CBHW021821270326
41932CB00007B/279